The Silver Spring Farm Cookbook

The Best of Garlic, Squash, Pumpkins and Onions

Published by Ottawa-Carleton Association
    for Persons with Developmental Disabilities
    880 Wellington Street, Suite 200, Ottawa, Ontario K1R 6K7
    (613) 569-8993 FAX (613) 569-9865

www.ocapdd.on.ca
ocapdd@ocapdd.on.ca

ISBN 1-894439-08-2
    Creative Bound International Inc., on behalf of Ottawa-Carleton
    Association for Persons with Developmental Disabilities
    Printed and bound in Canada

3rd printing © 2002, 2003 Ottawa-Carleton Association
    for Persons with Developmental Disabilities

Silver Spring Farm is an Official Mark of Ottawa-Carleton
    Association for Persons with Developmental Disabilities

Production by Creative Bound International Inc., *Publication Specialists*
    Gail Baird, Managing Editor
    Wendy O'Keefe, Designer

Cover photo © Getty Images
Back cover photos: barn: Jack Fraser
                    onions and garlic: Ted Davis

National Library of Canada Cataloguing in Publication Data

The Silver Spring Farm cookbook : the best of garlic, squash,
pumpkins and onions.

ISBN 1-894439-08-2

1. Cookery (Garlic) 2. Cookery (Onions) 3. Cookery (Squash)
4. Cookery (Pumpkin) I. Ottawa-Carleton Association for Persons with
Developmental Disabilities

TX801.S53 2002   641.6'525   C2002-903326-8

Love, encouragement and respect
are the ingredients needed to ensure
that all people reach their potential.

This book is dedicated to all persons
with developmental disabilities,
their families and their caregivers who
mix these ingredients together with
such perseverance and commitment.

Contents

Recipes

Appetizers and Spreads

Salads

Soups

Vegetables

Meat and Fish

Casseroles and Main Dishes

Pasta

Breads and Desserts

Acknowledgements

We wish to thank all our Silver Spring Farm customers who have visited us over the years and who have given us (many times over!) the suggestion for putting together a cookbook.

Such an endeavor could not have come to fruition without tremendous help, particularly in such areas as recipe collection, preparation and testing, and in data entry onto computer disk.

We wish to acknowledge those who have helped in any way with the Silver Spring Farm project. First and foremost are our volunteers who have laboured in the fields with the garlic, squash, pumpkin, gourd and red onion crops and who have helped harvest and sell the produce. We also thank those individuals and organizations that have made generous donations of money, food, equipment and supplies, and the media who continue to spread the good word that Silver Spring Farm produce is available to consumers.

• • •

Sometimes, a particular group of individuals go "above and beyond" in their commitment to help. Such a group is The Church of Jesus Christ of Latter-day Saints, with members from the Ottawa Ontario Stake, the Young Men and Young Women and their leaders, and the Humanitarian Services of Salt Lake City, Utah, Natalia and Gordon de Savigny and family, Patricia and Travis Tustian and Jeremy Waugh.

Many, many individuals, organizations and corporations have contributed to the success of Silver Spring Farm and our various projects. We are appreciative of all their abundant kindnesses. In alphabetical order, they are:

Peggy Adams	Kathleen and Bob Bigras
Carol Alette	Frances Bleeks
Peggy Amundson	George Braithwaite
Simon Arsenault	Anne and Andrew Bromley
Baird O'Keefe Publishing Inc.	Alma Brown
B & G Signs	Anne and Scott Brown
Barrhaven Independent	Ambrose Burnett
Angela Barkley	Calvin Burnett
Kelly Beasley	Don Burnside
Bell Canada	CBC Radio and TV
Bells Corners United Church	CJOH TV
Carl Bertrand	Sharon Channer

Patricia Chartrand
Gary Chivers
Christ Church (Anglican)
   Bells Corners
James Clark
J.J. Clarke and CJOH News
Rob Clipperton
Pam Collacott
Tom Conway and Family
Gay Cook
Bertie Coombs
Carol Cooper
Jim Craig
Kelly Crichton
Muriel Crosby
Ralph Dale Fertilizers
Donna Davidson
Ted Davis
Connie Defalco
Germaine Demers
Lilian de Savigny
Maria de Sousa
Matthew Dickson
Victor Dillabaugh
Grant Dillenbeck
Domus Café
Domus Housewares
Donley's Pool Services
Tori Dragon
Shirley Duncan
Cathy Dunn
Lois Dunn
Ron Eade
Norma Ednie
Cyndi Edwards and
   The NewRO News Team
John Emerson
Dale Esdaile
Gary Featherstone
Joan Fitch
Launi Fotopoulos
Steven Fouchard
Bertha Foulkes
Jim Fraser
Debbie Gasiecki
Gino's Garlic Farm
Gloucester-Nepean
   Professional Firefighters
   Association Benevolent Fund
Glengyle Garlic

Andrea Giamberardino
Floyd Granlund
Celia and Brian Grant
Green Door Restaurant
Victor Grostern
Ed Haines
Sheila Harris
Steve Harrison
Rena Hauver
Stuart Henry
Jane Hillbourne
Brenda House
Judi Huard
Al Hubenig
Betty Hudson
Nevil Hunt
Eileen Hyslop
Robbi Jordan
Kanata Kourier-Standard
Kanata Scouts
Darlene Keith
Angela Kirk
Helen Kirk
Laura Kirk
Rob Kirwan
Lacombe Toilet Rentals
Peter Larocque and Family
Myrna Laurenceson
Joanne Lee
Vera Legault
Bunny and Bob LeMessurier
Cecylia Lisiecki
Loblaws (Bells Corners)
Loeb (Bells Corners)
Loeb (Greenbank)
Dorothy Linden
John MacDonald
Mildred MacDonald
Angela Mangiacasale
Gene Markell
Serge Massey
Margaret Matheson
Jack McArton
Monica McGrath
Eleanor and Craig Mellish
Bob Mitchell
John Mitchell
Brian Moffatt
John Moore
Paul Morrisette

Wendy Morrison
Barbara Mottram
Lois Mundy
Leslie, Will and John Natynczyk
Margaret Natynczyk
National Capital Commission (NCC)
Nepean This Week
Terry Nichols
Barbara Nishimoto
Bonnie Norcott
Jean Oldfield
Ottawa Citizen
Allison Palmer
Rudy Parent
Parry Patton
Tim Porter
Mary Lou and Paul Pospisil
Liz Priestman
Rozalia Ratkiewicz
RBC Royal Bank
Rentalex (Stittsville)
Michelle Rickard
Marilyn Richardson
Marlene and Glenn Richardson
Richmond Nursery
Joan Riding
Ritchie's Feed and Seed
Syd Rolfe
Rotary Club of Nepean-Kanata
Gwen Rowbottom

William Sample
Ed Saunders
Wayne Senior
Francine Sim
Gary Skillen
Ann Smith
Sally Smith
S.O.S. Power Sales
Marilyn Spencer
Stittsville News
Wendy Storey
Heather Anne and Ken Stuyt
Ter-Mor Enterprises
The Herb Garden
The NewRO TV
The News
Tim Horton's (Bells Corners)
Bonnie Todd
Tramps Cafe
Barb Turner
Joan Turner
Hugh Urbach
Marnie Van Steen
Walter Baker Chapter I.O.D.E.
Doug Ward
West Carleton Review
Carole and Herb Westman
Brian Wilson
Michael Wollock
Anna Marie Young

We have made every effort to make sure this list is accurate and complete. If we have made an error, please accept our apologies and let us know so we may correct our records.

We quite simply don't know what we would do without you!

The Cookbook Committee:

Natalia de Savigny   Merle Fraser   Jack Fraser

Anne Mundy-Markell   Mary Frances Taylor

Ottawa-Carleton Association for
Persons with Developmental Disabilities

A Helping History...

Founded in 1950 and previously known as the Ottawa and District Association for the Mentally Retarded, the Ottawa-Carleton Association for Persons with Developmental Disabilities (OCAPDD) is the largest and longest-serving association of its kind in Ottawa. The organization had it origins in the determination of a small group of parents who believed that their children deserved access to education. Today, OCAPDD provides support to hundreds of persons with developmental disabilities, in every aspect of life whether seeking work opportunities, securing living arrangements or dealing with day-to-day tasks. Since fully a third of OCAPDD's clients are also affected by physical disabilities and other medical considerations, the scope of the organization's support is in direct response to level of need.

OCAPDD's management team oversees the operation of several residences, day programs and support services, which in turn are staffed by several hundred full-time and part-time employees who support individuals living either in family settings or independently. Residential programs are open 365 days a year, with night and relief staff playing a crucial role. A director is on call at all times.

A 12-person volunteer board of directors, which includes parents of persons with developmental disabilities, ensures the continued health of the Association. Board members are also tireless advocates on behalf of all persons with developmental disabilities.

Volunteers—a vital force in OCAPDD—contribute literally hundreds of hours each month in every conceivable activity, from organizing outings and tending gardens to servicing computers, mending clothes, and repairing and painting program facilities, to cite just a few examples.

Silver Spring Farm of Ottawa, Ontario

For a quarter of a century, children, youth and adults have made outings to picturesque Silver Spring Farm, located in the west end of Ottawa at the intersection of Richmond and Baseline Roads. There, through the auspices of the Ottawa-Carleton Association for Persons with Developmental Disabilities (OCAPDD), they have participated in activities and fundraising efforts supporting persons with developmental disabilities.

Silver Spring Farm claims a history all its own. Prior to becoming part of Ottawa-Carleton's Greenbelt through government expropriation in the 1960s, Silver Spring Farm was owned by a Dr. Moffat and operated as a major dairy farm. Thereafter, when OCAPDD entered into a long-term lease with the National Capital Commission for this piece of Greenbelt property, Moffat House, the original stone home and residence of Dr. Moffat and his family, became one of the first residences for OCAPDD clients. Since that time, two additional residences, Campbell House and Charette House, have been built on the property.

In the early days of the farm's operation by OCAPDD, the stables in the horse barn were rented out for riding school activities. Many visitors today still recall fondly their equestrian outings at Silver Spring Farm. Visits to the goats were reportedly also a highlight!

A tree nursery, later replaced by a greenhouse project, continued onsite until 1995. OCAPDD clients took great pride in actively participating in the growing of bedding plants and poinsettias. Silver Spring Farm plants had a wonderful reputation throughout the community, and no Christmas season was complete without a visit to buy a beautiful poinsettia. In the summers, OCAPDD clients sold corn and other vegetables at the roadside stand.

Throughout the 1980s and 1990s, spring water was also sold at the roadside. It was reputed to be the best-tasting water in the region, according to an *Ottawa Citizen* article in July 1982.

In 1996, a new project was begun. This initiative, which involved the growing of garlic, was one that would require much more volunteer support than past projects, and help was enlisted from the local community. The Church of Jesus Christ of Latter-day Saints has willingly provided a significant portion of the volunteers and equipment since that time, helping with the garlic, and later the squash, pumpkin, gourd and red onion crops. This volunteer base has further expanded through the support of members of the Ottawa-Carleton community. OCAPDD clients also play an active role in these activities in specific ways, such as separating the garlic cloves for fall planting and assisting with parts of the gardening, harvesting and planting activities.

From dairy farming to horseback riding, bedding plants and fresh spring water, and now boasting bountiful crops of garlic, squash, pumpkins and onions, this special property has made a unique contribution to the Ottawa-Carleton community throughout its history. While the nature of its role has evolved over the years, Silver Spring Farm remains a true Ottawa landmark in its support of persons with developmental disabilities.

Introduction

The Silver Spring Farm Cookbook is designed to introduce the reader to the wonderful uses of fresh garlic and onions in everyday cooking and to present the family of squash and pumpkins in such a way as to encourage their use in a variety of recipes. The recipes were submitted by various members of our community. All were tested beforehand and passed the taste test of many a family supper table.

The criteria by which recipes were selected for inclusion in this collection were ease of preparation, availability of ingredients in the average kitchen, and whether the end result would appeal to a wide range of tastes. We emphasize the use of fresh ingredients with minimal use of any packaged or prepared, canned or frozen foods.

Also included in *The Silver Spring Farm Cookbook* are planting, harvesting and storage instructions for those eager to try growing these vegetables in their own garden
.

We have made every effort to ensure the recipes in this book are accurate and complete. If we have made an error, please accept our apologies and let us know.

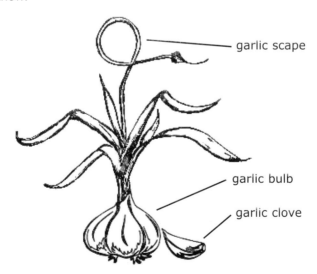

garlic scape

garlic bulb

garlic clove

May you find some lasting cooking traditions
to enjoy for many years to come!

Appetizers and Spreads

Whipped Garlic Butter

Yield: approximately 1 cup

  1 cup butter, softened
  4 garlic cloves, crushed
  1 teaspoon dried parsley (optional)

Beat butter and garlic in a small bowl until light and fluffy and store in an airtight container in the refrigerator for up to 1 week. Serve with hot rolls, bread, rice or cooked vegetables.

For a quick way to make garlic bread, simply butter both cut sides of your loaf with the whipped garlic butter. Cover with foil and bake at 350°F until bread is heated through, 15–30 minutes depending on the size of your loaf.

• • •

Herbed Garlic Butter

Yield: approximately 1 cup

  1 cup butter, softened
  2 tablespoons fresh parsley, chopped or 1 teaspoon dried
  4–5 garlic cloves, chopped
  1 tablespoon onion flakes
  1/2 tablespoon lemon juice
  dash pepper

Mix all ingredients together and store in a covered container or rolled in foil wrap. It will keep in the refrigerator for up to 1 week.

Use to make garlic bread or as a flavoured butter for cooked vegetables.

Roasted Garlic Butter   Yield: approximately 1/2 cup

    4 large garlic bulbs
    4 tablespoons olive oil
    4 teaspoons water
    3 tablespoons butter, softened
    2–3 drops Tabasco sauce
    salt and pepper to taste

1. Remove any loose papery skin from the garlic bulbs. Slice off the tips of garlic bulbs to expose a little garlic flesh. Place in a small ovenproof dish and drizzle with olive oil and water. Cover with foil. Bake in 350°F oven for 30–45 minutes or until flesh is soft.

2. When garlic is cool enough to handle, squeeze the flesh from each clove into a small bowl. Add any remaining pan juices and mash garlic with a fork. Blend with butter, Tabasco sauce, salt and pepper.

3. Serve at room temperature with crusty bread or crackers.

Can be stored in the refrigerator for up to 2 weeks.

The roasted garlic takes on a wonderful caramel-like nutty taste.

Roasted Garlic Spread   Yield: 1/4–1/3 cup

1 whole garlic bulb
2 tablespoons olive oil
2 teaspoons chopped fresh herbs, such as parsley,
    thyme, chives or tarragon
salt and pepper to taste

1. Cut off the top of the garlic bulb just enough to expose the flesh. Brush the garlic bulb with olive oil enough to cover generously. Reserve remaining olive oil. Wrap garlic bulb in foil and place in a small baking dish.

2. Bake at 375°F for 30–45 minutes or until flesh is soft.

3. Cool garlic bulb enough to touch and squeeze out the garlic flesh into a small bowl. Stir in remaining olive oil and herbs, and season with salt and pepper.

As this is a very small baking item, it is more practical and efficient to use a toaster oven, if possible. The smell emanating from the roasting garlic is exquisite. Use on fresh crusty bread as an appetizer or as a flavouring in a meat or vegetable dish. Keeps up to 1 week in the refrigerator.

Basil and Oil Dip

Yield: approximately 1 1/3 cups

1/2 cup olive oil
1/2 cup fresh basil, chopped
8 garlic cloves, chopped
1/4 cup balsamic vinegar
1 teaspoon red chili flakes (more if you prefer hotter)
crusty or sourdough bread, cut into 1" cubes

1. Mix together the olive oil, basil, garlic, vinegar and red chili flakes, and place in a shallow dish so as to have approximately 1/4" depth of mixture. Let stand approximately 10 minutes.

2. Serve alongside a plateful of bread cubes.

For an extra special presentation, decorate with a few snips of pansy or nasturtium flowers fresh from your garden. Snip the flowers, discard the stems and let the flowers float on top of dip. You may eat the flowers, too, if you wish!

• • •

Garlic Stuffed Mushroom Caps

Serves 4–6

2 large shredded wheat biscuits, crushed into fine meal
2 garlic cloves, finely chopped
2 tablespoons melted butter
1/4 cup cheddar cheese (medium or old), grated
24–36 large mushroom caps (stems removed)
salt and pepper to taste

1. Place crushed shredded wheat in a medium bowl.

2. In a small frying pan, sauté garlic in melted butter for 3–4 minutes over medium heat and drizzle over the shredded wheat.

3. Add grated cheese and stir until mixture sticks together.

4. Press a spoonful into each mushroom cap.

5. Place on baking sheet and broil in oven until crispy and browned.

Hummus   Yield: approximately 2 cups

1 can chickpeas (540 ml or 19 oz.), drained
   or 2/3 cup dried chickpeas which have been
   soaked, cooked and drained
2 garlic cloves, peeled and left whole
juice of 1 lemon
1/2 teaspoon salt or to taste
1/4 cup tahini (ground sesame), optional
1/4 cup olive oil

1. To prepare dried chickpeas, discard any that are spoiled. Rinse several times. Place chickpeas in a large bowl. Cover with water and let soak overnight. The following day, transfer chickpeas to large stockpot and add water to cover. Bring to a boil, then simmer for 1 1/2 to 2 hours or until chickpeas are tender. Drain.

2 In a food processor, purée all ingredients except olive oil. With food processor turned on, slowly feed oil through tube until mixture forms a smooth paste. It should have the consistency of thick mayonnaise. If using tahini, you may have to add a little more lemon juice.

3. Serve with pita bread.

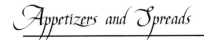

Hummus with Roasted Garlic   Yield: approximately 2 cups

1 whole garlic bulb
1 teaspoon olive oil
1 onion, coarsely chopped
1/4 cup olive oil
1 teaspoon ground coriander
1/2 teaspoon ground cumin
1/4 teaspoon freshly ground black pepper
pinch turmeric
pinch cayenne pepper
1 can chickpeas (540 ml or 19 oz.), drained but reserving some
    liquid or 2 cups cooked chickpeas from 2/3 cup dried (see
    Hummus recipe, page 21)
3 tablespoons lemon juice
1 teaspoon salt or to taste

1. Remove papery outer skin of garlic bulb. Cut off tips of garlic bulb leaving some garlic flesh exposed. In a small baking dish, sprinkle garlic bulb with 1 teaspoon of olive oil. Enclose bulb in foil. Bake in toaster oven or regular oven at 350°F for 30–45 minutes or until flesh is soft.

2. Sauté the onion in 1/4 cup olive oil until softened, about 3–4 minutes. Over low heat, add spices and cook gently for another 3–4 minutes. Remove from heat.

3. When garlic is done and cool enough to handle, squeeze out the pulp and add to the onion mixture.

4. Purée onion mixture, drained chickpeas, lemon juice and salt in food processor until smooth. If mixture is too dry, add chickpea water or plain water, a little at a time to achieve desired consistency. Serve chilled or at room temperature.

A nice twist to hummus.

Hummus with Feta
Yield: approximately 2 1/4 cups

2 garlic cloves, peeled and left whole
1 can chickpeas (540 ml or 19 oz.), drained and rinsed or 2 cups
    cooked chickpeas from 2/3 cup dried (see Hummus recipe,
    page 21)
1 tomato, quartered
1/4 cup feta cheese
2 tablespoons lemon juice
1 tablespoon olive oil
salt and pepper to taste

In food processor, add garlic, chickpeas, tomato and feta cheese. Process until smooth. With machine running, pour lemon juice and oil through tube. Season to taste with salt and pepper. May have to add more oil and/or lemon juice to achieve a consistency similar to that of mayonnaise.

Serve with pita bread or crackers.

For a lighter dip, you may substitute light sour cream or yogurt for the feta.

• • •

Garlic Artichoke Dip
Yield: approximately 2 1/4 cups

1 can artichoke hearts (398 ml) finely chopped
    —keep 3/4 of the liquid
3/4 cup Parmesan cheese (use freshly grated for best flavour)
1/2 cup salad dressing
1 whole garlic bulb with cloves peeled and chopped

1. Mix artichoke, liquid, Parmesan cheese, salad dressing and garlic in a medium bowl.
2. Spoon into a shallow baking dish and bake at 350°F for 15 minutes or until mixture is bubbling.
3. Serve with crackers or bread.

You'll want more!

Red Pepper Dip

Yield: approximately 1 1/2 cups

3 large red peppers
2 garlic cloves, peeled and left whole
2 teaspoons lemon juice
1 pkg cream cheese (250 g), cubed
salt and pepper to taste

1. Broil the whole peppers on a cookie sheet, turning every few minutes until the skin is blackened and blistered and no longer red, approximately 20–25 minutes. The peppers can also be roasted over the barbecue on medium heat. After peppers have been blackened, place in a covered casserole and let sit for 5–10 minutes.

2. Peel off outer skin. Cut peppers in half and discard insides.

3. In food processor, purée the peppers, garlic and lemon juice. Through feeder of food processor with machine running, gradually add the cubes of cream cheese and process until smooth. Season with salt and pepper. Allow flavours to blend for at least a few hours before serving.

Truly a beautifully coloured dip. Serve with your choice of fresh vegetables, fresh crusty bread or crackers.

• • •

Garlic Scape Dip

Yield: 1 1/4 cups

1/2 cup sour cream
1/2 cup mayonnaise
1 1/2 tablespoons fresh dill, chopped fine (or 1 teaspoon dried dill)
2-3 garlic scapes,* chopped fine or 1 clove garlic, finely chopped
1 tablespoon white vinegar

Mix together, and if desired, thin with milk.

If you would prefer a lighter version of this dip, simply replace up to half of the sour cream and mayonnaise with plain yogurt.

Wonderful with veggies!

* Note: See Page 150 for garlic scape information.

Broccoli Spread
Yield: approximately 2 cups

2 cups broccoli, cut into 2" pieces
1/3 cup onion, coarsely chopped
1-2 garlic cloves, coarsely chopped
1/4 teaspoon crushed red pepper
2 tablespoons olive oil
2 tablespoons grated Parmesan cheese

1. In saucepan, cook broccoli in small amount of water until just tender. Drain but reserve the vegetable water.
2. In small frying pan, cook onion, garlic and red pepper in olive oil until onion is soft, approximately 10 minutes.
3. Combine cooked broccoli, onion mixture and Parmesan cheese in food processor. Blend until smooth and creamy. May have to add slightly more oil and reserved broccoli water if mixture looks too dry.
4. Serve at room temperature with pita bread or crackers.

• • •

Garlic Cottage Cheese Spread
Yield: approximately 1 cup

1 cup cottage cheese
2 garlic cloves, chopped
1/4 teaspoon thyme
1/4 teaspoon marjoram
1/4 teaspoon pepper

1. In food processor, mix all the above ingredients until smooth. Store in the refrigerator until ready to serve.
2. Serve with your choice of crackers or vegetables.

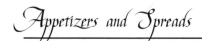

Garlic, Onion and Herb Pita Chips

Yield: 80 wedges

5 whole wheat or white 6" pita breads
1/2 cup extra virgin olive oil
2 garlic cloves, finely chopped
1 green onion, finely chopped
1 tablespoon parsley, finely chopped
1 1/2 tablespoons finely chopped fresh herbs of
    choice, e.g. basil, dill, rosemary, etc.
grated Parmesan cheese (optional)

1. Mix garlic, onion, parsley and fresh herbs with oil and let sit for at least 1 hour to allow flavours to blend

2. Preheat oven to 350°F . Split each pita bread horizontally to make 2 halves. Lightly brush the entire lighter-textured surface of each half with the oil mixture. Cut each half into 8 wedges. Sprinkle with cheese (optional).

3. Place on cookie sheets and bake for approximately 6–7 minutes until golden brown. (Watch closely as oven temperatures and time can vary). Store in airtight container in refrigerator.

Serve with dips, or enjoy as chips. These will disappear quickly!

• • •

Roasted Pumpkin Seeds

Yield: 1/2 cup

1/2 cup pumpkin seeds
1 teaspoon vegetable oil
salt or flavoured salt

1. Remove seeds from fresh pumpkin and separate away the stringy fibre. Wash the seeds under cold water and pat dry between layers of paper towels.

2. In a small bowl, mix together the pumpkin seeds and oil and add enough salt to sprinkle seeds well.

Roasted Pumpkin Seeds, *continued*

3. Spread seeds on a flat baking sheet in a single layer and bake at 350°F for approximately 20 minutes or until the seeds take on a nice golden colour. Taste and adjust seasonings if necessary. Cool.

The bigger jack-o'-lantern pumpkins will have the bigger seeds but you can also roast seeds using the smaller cooking pumpkins and even squash. The seeds roast quite nicely in your toaster oven.

• • •

Salsa   Yield: approximately 3 cups

4 large tomatoes, chopped (and seeded, if you prefer)
1/4 cup green onions, chopped (white or red onion
  may also be used)
1/4 cup cilantro or parsley, chopped
1 tablespoon basil or oregano
1–2 garlic cloves, chopped
1 teaspoon chopped jalapeño peppers or
  1/2 teaspoon chili flakes or 1 teaspoon hot sauce
2 tablespoons olive oil
juice of 1/2 lime or lemon
1 teaspoon sugar
1 teaspoon salt

Mix all ingredients and allow to stand at least 1 hour for flavours to blend.

Serve with tortilla chips or crackers as a dip, over hot spaghetti, chicken breast or with fillet of fish.

Using Roma tomatoes will make your salsa less watery.

Broiled Garlic Pita Wedges   Serves 3–4

1/3 cup olive oil
1 garlic clove, chopped
2 tablespoons fresh parsley, chopped
5 whole wheat or white 6" pita breads, cut into quarters
3 tablespoons grated Parmesan cheese

1. In small bowl, combine oil, garlic and parsley. Brush part of the mixture over one side of the pita bread quarters and place onto an ungreased cookie sheet.

2. Broil approximately 1–2 minutes or until edges turn slightly golden. Remove cookie sheet from oven, turn bread over and brush the other side with the remaining oil mixture.

3. Broil 1–2 minutes longer or until golden and crisp.

4. Place on serving platter and sprinkle with Parmesan cheese.

If you let the oil mixture sit for up to 1 hour, the flavours will have blended to give you extra garlic taste. Try this over the barbecue, as well, but watch carefully. Great with hummus, soups or salads.

• • •

Broiled Pita with Garlic and Cumin   Serves 6

4 teaspoons olive oil
1–2 garlic cloves, chopped fine
1/4 teaspoon cumin
1/4 teaspoon black pepper
3 whole wheat or white 6" pita breads

In a small bowl, combine the olive oil, garlic, cumin and pepper. Brush over the bread on one side and broil for 1–2 minutes or until lightly browned. Repeat on other side.

Cut into wedges and serve with salad or soup.

Squash with Lime and Coconut   Yield: approximately 30 cubes

1 butternut squash (approximately 2 lb. or 1 kg size),
   and cut into 1/2" cubes
2 tablespoons butter
2 garlic cloves, sliced
2 tablespoons shredded coconut
1 tablespoon lime juice
1 teaspoon finely grated lime peel
dash hot pepper sauce
salt to taste

1. Fill medium pot 1/3 full of water and add squash cubes. Bring to a boil and simmer until almost fork tender, approximately 4 minutes. Drain well.

2. In non-stick frying pan, brown coconut over medium-low heat until it turns a nice light brown colour. Remove from heat and set aside in a small dish.

3. In same frying pan, melt butter. Add garlic and cook stirring 1 minute. Remove garlic and discard, leaving the flavour in the pan. Add cooked squash to pan and cook until golden on all sides, approximately 8 minutes. Remove from heat.

4. Add coconut, lime juice, lime peel and hot pepper sauce. Toss to coat evenly. Salt to taste.

5. Arrange on a platter with the squash cubes skewered with toothpicks. Serve at room temperature.

Sure to be a hit with your guests—not too many will have tried squash like this!

Bruschetta   Serves 4

    6 tomatoes, chopped
    3 green onions, chopped approximately 1/4 cup
    1/4 cup fresh basil, chopped
    1/2 cup mozzarella, shredded
    2 garlic cloves, chopped
    3 tablespoons balsamic vinegar
    1 tablespoon + 1 teaspoon olive oil
    1/4 teaspoon black pepper
    12 slices Italian bread, 1/2" thick

1. Place tomatoes, green onions, basil, cheese and garlic in a large bowl. Stir to mix.

2. Place vinegar and oil in a small bowl and mix well. Add to tomato mixture with black pepper. Cover and let stand at room temperature until ready to spread on bread.

3. Arrange bread slices in a single layer on a baking sheet. Bake at 400°F for 3–5 minutes or until lower side is golden brown. Turn slices over and bake another 3 minutes or so to brown other side. To add extra garlic flavor, rub peeled garlic clove over toasted bread.

4. Spoon tomato mixture over each slice and serve immediately.

Eating this can be messy, so you may want to finish it off with a knife and fork!

Salads

Spinach Salad with Roasted Garlic   Serves 4

     1 whole garlic bulb
     1 tablespoon olive oil
     5–6 slices of French bread, 1" thick, toasted
     1 tablespoon olive oil
     1 1/2 tablespoons lemon juice
     3 tablespoons olive oil
     1 cup mozzarella cheese, grated
     dash white sugar
     1/2 bag spinach (150 g or 5 oz.), washed with stems removed

1. Cut off tip of garlic bulb to leave top flesh exposed and place in a small baking dish.

2. Sprinkle with 1 tablespoon of olive oil and cover with foil. Bake in toaster oven or regular oven at 350°F for 35–40 minutes. Cool slightly.

3. Squeeze out the roasted garlic flesh and mix 1/2 of the garlic flesh with 1 tablespoon of olive oil. Spread over one side of the toasted French bread. Cut bread into cubes and toast lightly in a medium frying pan for a few minutes. (Reserve the other half of the roasted garlic for the salad dressing.)

4. Mix together the lemon juice, 3 tablespoons of olive oil, mozzarella, dash of sugar and the reserved garlic flesh.

5. Just before serving, toss together the spinach with the salad dressing and bread cubes.

Caesar Salad   Serves 8

    2 cups day-old French, Italian or egg bread, cubed
    2 tablespoons olive oil
    1 teaspoon black pepper
    1/4 cup lemon juice, approximately 1 lemon
    2 garlic cloves, crushed
    1 teaspoon anchovy paste
    1 teaspoon Dijon mustard
    1 teaspoon Worcestershire sauce
    dash Tabasco sauce
    1/4 teaspoon salt
    1/4 teaspoon pepper
    1/2 cup olive oil
    1 large head romaine lettuce, torn into bite-size pieces
    1/2 cup grated Parmesan cheese (freshly grated is best)
    1/2 cup bacon bits (optional)

1. To toast croutons, use day-old French, Italian or egg bread. Cut bread into 1/2" cubes and place in a medium bowl. Sprinkle with olive oil and a very generous grinding of black pepper. Bake on cookie sheet in preheated 350°F oven; stirring occasionally until lightly toasted, approximately 13–15 minutes. Cool.

2. In small bowl, whisk lemon juice, garlic, anchovy paste, Dijon mustard, Worcestershire sauce, Tabasco sauce, salt and pepper. Gradually whisk in olive oil. Cover and refrigerate. Dressing may be made several days in advance. It is best to prepare dressing at least 1 hour before serving.

3. Toss lettuce with dressing in a large salad bowl. Add croutons and Parmesan cheese and toss again. Serve immediately.

Croutons can be stored in airtight container for several days if they last that long!

For extra garlic taste, marinate one clove of coarsely chopped garlic in 2 tablespoons of olive oil for approximately 30 minutes and sprinkle onto the bread cubes.

Caesar Salad, *continued*

For even more garlic taste, cut the bread into thick slices and toast. Rub peeled garlic clove over toasted bread and then cut into cubes and follow crouton recipe.

• • •

Green Bean Salad

Serves 4–6

    1 lb. green beans, whole with tips trimmed (approximately 500 g)
    1 sweet red pepper, cut into thin strips
    1/3 cup olive or vegetable oil
    3 tablespoons red wine vinegar
    1 garlic clove, chopped fine
    1 tablespoon fresh basil, chopped, or 1 teaspoon dried
    2 teaspoons Dijon mustard
    1/2 teaspoon sugar
    1/2 teaspoon salt or to taste

1. Cook beans in a small amount of water for 4–5 minutes or until tender-crisp.

2. Drain cooking water. Run beans under cold water and drain once again. Cover and refrigerate until ready to use.

3. Combine the oil, vinegar, garlic, basil, mustard, sugar and salt.

4. Pour onto the red pepper strips and marinate in the refrigerator for 30 minutes or overnight.

5. Just before serving stir in the green beans.

You can substitute green beans with cauliflower and/or broccoli. The pepper adds wonderful contrast.

Broccoli Salad   Serves 4–6

4 cups fresh broccoli, cut into bite-size pieces
1/2 cup chopped red onion
1/2 cup sunflower seeds
1/2 cup raisins
5 strips bacon, fried and crumbled
1/4 cup feta cheese (optional) crumbled,
      or cheddar cheese (optional) shredded
1/4 cup plain, low-fat yogurt
1/4 cup light mayonnaise or salad dressing
2–4 teaspoons sugar
1 tablespoon lemon juice or vinegar
salt and pepper to taste

1. In large bowl, combine broccoli, onion, sunflower seeds, raisins, bacon and cheese.

2 In a small bowl, stir together the yogurt, mayonnaise, sugar, lemon juice, salt and pepper.

3. Pour over salad and toss to mix. Cover and refrigerate for several hours.

An additional 1/4 cup of mayonnaise or salad dressing may be substituted for yogurt.

This salad is always a hit!

Marinated Eggplant Salad   Serves 5

1/4 cup olive oil
1 medium eggplant, peeled and cut into 1/2" cubes
3 sweet peppers, red and/or green, cut into 1/2" cubes
1 dried chili pepper, crushed
1 medium onion, diced
1 cup celery, cut into 1/2" cubes
2 garlic cloves, chopped
1/2 teaspoon dried basil
1/2 teaspoon dried oregano
1/2 teaspoon dried thyme
3/4 cup red wine vinegar
1 cup black olives, pitted and quartered
1/4 cup fresh parsley, chopped
1 tablespoon sugar
2 tablespoons lemon juice
1 garlic clove, chopped

1. In a large frying pan, sauté eggplant in olive oil for several minutes. Add sweet peppers, chili pepper and onion, and continue to cook for approximately 2 minutes. Add celery, chopped garlic and the dried herbs, and continue to cook for several minutes.

2. Add vinegar and cook until the vinegar boils. Remove from heat and stir in the olives, parsley, sugar, lemon juice and one clove of chopped garlic.

3. Marinate in a covered container in the refrigerator overnight.

4. Enjoy it with some thickly sliced crusty bread.

This salad is probably best enjoyed by the adult crowd.

Middle Eastern Chickpea Salad   Serves 4

1 can chickpeas (540 ml or 19 oz.), rinsed and drained
4 green onions, thinly sliced
1 small green pepper, chopped
1 tomato, seeded and chopped
1/4 cup chopped fresh parsley
1/4 cup lemon juice (approximately 1 whole lemon)
1 garlic clove, crushed
1/2 cup olive oil
1/4 teaspoon ground cumin
salt and pepper to taste
lemon slices and black olives for garnish

Combine chickpeas, green onions, green pepper, tomato and parsley. Whisk lemon juice, garlic, olive oil, cumin, salt and pepper together until well blended and add to vegetables. Salads is best marinated in the refrigerator for 30 minutes.

Serve salad in a flat bowl or dish surrounded with lemon slices. Top with black olives.

This is an excellent picnic salad.

Couscous Salad   Serves 4

    1 cup instant regular couscous
    1 cup boiling water
    1 tablespoon olive oil
    1/4 teaspoon salt
    1/2 cucumber, chopped
    1-2 garlic cloves, finely chopped
    1 fresh or pickled chili pepper, finely chopped
    1/4-1/2 cup green onions, finely chopped
    2 tomatoes, chopped
    1/2 teaspoon salt or to taste
    1/4 cup chopped coriander or parsley
    1/4 cup chopped mint leaves (optional)
    juice of 1/2 lemon
    1/4 cup olive oil
    1 teaspoon pepper

Add hot water to couscous in a medium bowl with 1 tablespoon of olive oil and 1/4 teaspoon of salt. Stir and allow to swell, approximately 2-3 minutes. Allow to cool, stirring occasionally.

When cool, add remaining ingredients. Serve or store in refrigerator until ready to serve.

Very easy to make.

Orange Balsamic Couscous Salad   Serves 6

    1 cup instant regular couscous
    1 cup boiling water
    1/2 cup hot orange juice
    2 stalks celery, finely chopped
    1 red pepper, chopped
    2 green onions, thinly sliced
    2 tablespoons balsamic vinegar
    1 teaspoon grated orange peel
    1 garlic clove, finely chopped
    1/4 cup olive oil
    salt and pepper to taste

1. Place couscous in a large bowl. Pour in hot water and juice and mix thoroughly. Let stand for 5 minutes. Fluff with a fork and let cool for 10 minutes.

2. Prepare vegetables and add to couscous mixture.

3. In a small bowl, stir balsamic vinegar with orange peel, garlic, salt and pepper. Whisk in olive oil and drizzle over couscous mixture. Toss to combine.

This salad may be eaten immediately or stored in the refrigerator to enhance flavour. If salad appears too dry, add a little more vinegar and oil.

Pasta Primavera Salad   Serves 4–6

2 cups uncooked pasta shells or penne
1 tablespoon olive oil
2–3 garlic cloves, chopped
1 cup sliced mushrooms
2 cups asparagus, cut into 1" pieces
1 cup green peas, fresh or frozen
3 medium tomatoes, chopped
1/4 cup fresh basil, chopped
3 tablespoons olive oil
3 tablespoons fresh lemon juice
1/2 cup freshly grated Parmesan cheese
1/4 cup fresh parsley, chopped
1/2 cup thinly sliced sun-dried tomatoes (optional)
lettuce as required
salt and pepper to taste

1. Cook the pasta in boiling salted water until al dente. Drain and rinse with cold water and set aside.

2. In medium frying pan, sauté the garlic in olive oil for 1 minute. Add the mushrooms and continue to cook over medium heat until just tender. Remove from heat and set aside.

3. Steam the asparagus and peas until tender.

4. Toss all the vegetables with the pasta. Add the rest of the ingredients and toss well.

5. Add more olive oil if needed and adjust seasonings to taste.

6. Serve warm or at room temperature on lettuce, with extra Parmesan to taste.

You may substitute bite-size pieces of broccoli or cauliflower or julienne carrots or celery for the asparagus and peas.

Beet Salad

Serves 4

4 medium beets, unpeeled, with tops removed
2–3 garlic cloves, finely chopped
2 tablespoons olive oil
1 teaspoon sugar
1 tablespoon lemon juice
salt and pepper to taste

1. Wash beets and place in pot covered with cold water. Cook over medium-low heat until beets are tender, approximately 40 minutes. Beets are done when you remove a beet and skin peels easily when rubbed. If beets are pierced, the juices bleed into the water.

2. Drain beets and allow to cool until not too hot to the touch. Peel and slice or cut into wedges.

3. Toss beets with garlic, olive oil, sugar, lemon juice and seasonings, and allow mixture to sit for one hour at room temperature. This salad tastes best served at room temperature.

• • •

Garlic Balsamic Dressing

Yield: approximately 1/4 cup

1 tablespoon balsamic or red-wine vinegar
1/2 teaspoon Dijon mustard
1 garlic clove, crushed
3 tablespoons olive oil
generous pinches of basil, oregano and hot red pepper flakes

Mix all ingredients together well. Serve with green salad of your choice.

Dill Vinaigrette   Yield: approximately 1 1/4 cups

2/3 cup vegetable oil
1/3 cup cider vinegar
1 garlic clove, crushed
1/2 tablespoon lemon juice
1 3/4 tablespoons brown sugar
1/4 teaspoon dry mustard
1/2 tablespoon dill weed
1/4 teaspoon salt
black pepper to taste

In a small bowl or jar, combine all ingredients and whisk or shake well.

Ideal for green salads. This is a great salad dressing to have on hand, as it keeps for a long time in your refrigerator.

• • •

Garlic and Maple Vinaigrette   Yield: approximately 1/2 cup

1/3 cup olive oil
1-2 garlic cloves, cut into several pieces
2 tablespoons lemon juice
1 tablespoon maple syrup
1 teaspoon Dijon mustard
salt to taste

Marinate garlic pieces in olive oil for at least several hours in the refrigerator. Remove garlic from the olive oil and discard. To the oil add the lemon juice, maple syrup and mustard. Whisk together.

Serve with leafy green salad of your choice.

If an enhanced garlic flavour is desired, chop the garlic finely and leave it in the salad dressing.

Salads

Balsamic Splash Vinaigrette

Yield: approximately 1/4 cup

>   3 tablespoons balsamic vinegar
>   2 tablespoons olive oil
>   1 tablespoon chicken broth or water
>   1 garlic clove, crushed
>   1 teaspoon mustard seed
>   1/2 teaspoon mustard powder
>   1/4 teaspoon liquid honey
>   salt and pepper to taste

In a small bowl or jar combine all ingredients and whisk or shake well.

Good with green salads, chicken dishes, cold sliced chicken or roast pork.

• • •

Red Onion Vinaigrette

Yield: approximately 3 1/2 cups

>   1 medium red onion, peeled and quartered
>   1 teaspoon dry mustard
>   1/2 teaspoon salt
>   1 cup white sugar
>   1/2 cup white vinegar
>   2 cups salad oil
>   2 teaspoons celery seed (optional)

In food processor, blend together the red onion, mustard, salt, sugar and vinegar. Slowly add the oil through the feeder tube and blend well. Stir in the celery seed.

Store in a covered container in the refrigerator for up to 3 weeks. Shake well before using.

This salad dressing is rather thick in consistency with a unique pinkish colour. A great salad dressing for greens as it adheres well.

Soups

Soup Tips

In general, soups are very simple to prepare and can often act as a main meal when served with bread and salad.

While, for the most part, they require a little preparation time, the flavours will blend better the longer the soup simmers.

Do not discard any precious vegetable cooking water. It is full of vitamins. Keep a container of vegetable broth handy in your freezer for use in soups or sauces.

Water and chicken, beef or vegetable bouillon may be used as a substitute for stock. An end rind of Parmesan cheese may be added and simmered with soup.

Homemade Meat Stock

1. Peel and slice one onion in half widthwise and char the cut side directly over the stove element over high heat until black.

2. Place onion in a stockpot, along with meat bones of your choice, cooked or raw. Bring to a boil with a little salt and remove the foam that floats to top. Simmer for at least 1 hour until meat comes off the bones.

3. Remove bones and pick off any meat. Return the meat to the soup or save for use in other recipes.

4. The easiest way to remove any fat from the stock is to chill the stock in the refrigerator and discard the fat that has solidified on top. A quicker method, if one is pressed for time, is to simply spoon off the fat floating on the surface of the stock.

5. Use the stock in your favourite soup recipes or freeze for future use.

Butternut Squash Soup   Serves 6–8

4 cups cold water
5 cups butternut squash, cut into 1" pieces
2 tablespoons butter
1 garlic clove, chopped
1 large onion, chopped
1 small red pepper, chopped
4 cups chicken stock*
1 cup cream**
1/2 teaspoon nutmeg
1/4–1/2 teaspoon cumin (to taste)
pinch of ginger
salt and pepper to taste

1. In a large saucepan, bring water to a boil. Add squash and cook covered for approximately 10 minutes, until just tender. Drain and set aside in a bowl.

2. In same saucepan, sauté garlic, onion and red pepper in butter, stirring for 3–5 minutes, until softened.

3. Stir in squash and chicken stock and bring to a boil. Reduce heat and simmer, partially covered, for 20 minutes, stirring occasionally.

4. Purée squash mixture in batches, using blender or food processor.

5. Return mixture to saucepan and stir in cream. Cook for 5 minutes.

6. Add nutmeg, cumin, ginger, salt and pepper. Taste and adjust seasonings if required.

* if using a powdered stock, the drained water from the cooked squash may be used.

** Although this recipe calls for cream, you can use any milk, skim, 1%, 2%, or homogenized, depending on your taste preference or to produce a lighter calorie, but still tasty, version.

Ginger Squash Soup   Serves 4

1 tablespoon butter
1 large onion, chopped
2 garlic cloves, chopped
4 teaspoons minced gingerroot, or 1 teaspoon dried
2 tablespoons flour
3 cups chicken stock
2 cups squash or pumpkin, cooked and mashed
1/2 cup cream or milk
1 teaspoon grated orange zest
dash nutmeg
salt and pepper to taste
2 tablespoons chopped parsley or chives

1. In medium saucepan, melt butter. Sauté onion, garlic, and ginger for approximately 5 minutes or until onions are softened. Add flour and mix well. Stir in stock and squash. Bring to a boil. Cover and simmer, approximately 10 minutes.

2. Purée soup. Add cream and orange zest. Season with salt, pepper and nutmeg.

3. Serve sprinkled with parsley or chives.

The ginger gives this soup a delicate spicy taste. Young children may not fancy it, but it should prove to be a hit when entertaining adults.

Harvest Pumpkin Soup   Serves 4

1 tablespoon butter or oil
1/2 cup onion, chopped
1/2 cup red or green bell pepper, finely chopped
2 1/2 cups chicken stock
1 medium potato, peeled and cubed
2/3 cup whole kernel corn, canned or frozen
1 1/4 cups squash or pumpkin, cooked and mashed
1/4 teaspoon pepper
1/4 teaspoon cumin
salt to taste

1. In medium saucepan, sauté onion and bell pepper with butter or oil until onion is soft, approximately 5 minutes.

2. Add stock, potato and corn, and bring to a boil. Decrease heat to low. Cover and simmer for approximately 5 minutes.

3. Add pumpkin, pepper, cumin and salt to stock mixture. Heat through and serve.

This soup is a wonderful rich colour.

Pumpkin Bisque   Serves 4

2 tablespoons butter
1/2 cup onion, chopped
1/4 cup celery, chopped
2 tablespoons celery leaves, chopped
1 1/2 cups pumpkin or squash, cooked and mashed
4 cups chicken or vegetable stock
1 teaspoon salt
1/8 teaspoon pepper
1 small bay leaf
1/4 teaspoon marjoram, dried
1/4 teaspoon thyme, dried
1/4–1/2 cup cream or milk

1. Melt butter in a medium saucepan. Add onion, celery and celery leaves. Cook mixture over low heat until vegetables are tender, approximately 5–7 minutes.

2. Stir in pumpkin, chicken stock and seasonings. Bring to a boil. Lower heat and simmer, uncovered, for approximately 45 minutes, stirring occasionally. Discard bay leaf.

3. Stir in cream or milk, and cook until heated through.

This soup will definitely be a hit with everyone!

Squash and Leek Soup   Serves 6

1/4 cup butter
1 large onion, chopped
2 leeks, white part only, chopped
1 large potato, peeled and diced
2 medium carrots, peeled and sliced
2 cups squash, peeled and diced
3 cups chicken stock
2 cups milk
salt and pepper to taste

1. Melt butter in a saucepan over medium heat and sauté the onion and leeks until soft. Add potato, carrots and squash. Add stock. Cover and simmer for approximately 20 minutes or until vegetables are tender.

2. Purée the soup, using hand blender or food processor. Stir in the milk and seasonings and heat through before serving.

The orange flecks from the chopped carrot give this soup a wonderful colour.

Curried Cream of Pumpkin Soup   Serves 8

1/4 cup butter
1 medium onion, chopped
3 garlic cloves, chopped
3 teaspoons garam masala
1/2 teaspoon pepper
2 teaspoons salt
1/4 cup flour
3 cups chicken or vegetable broth
3 cups pumpkin, peeled and chopped
1 large potato, chopped
3/4 cup table cream or milk
salt and pepper to taste

1. In a large saucepan, sauté onion and garlic in butter together with the garam marsala, pepper and salt on low heat for approximately 10 minutes.

2. Stir flour into onion and garlic mixture and mix well.

3. Gradually stir in broth, followed by the pumpkin and potato. Bring to a boil and then reduce heat and simmer for approximately 30–40 minutes.

4. Remove from heat. Using a hand blender or potato masher, purée soup until smooth.

5. Add cream and simmer on low heat for another few minutes or until heated through. Add salt and pepper to taste.

Garlic Soup with Roasted Vegetables   Serves 6

1 large pepper squash
1 medium onion, peeled and quartered
2 garlic bulbs
4 cups vegetable stock
1 medium beet (optional)
1/4 cup sour cream or plain yogurt
salt and pepper to taste

1. Cut squash in half lengthwise, removing seeds and stringy flesh. Place cut side down in a baking dish. Tuck onion quarters under the squash.

2. Cut off the tips of garlic bulbs leaving flesh exposed. Wrap the bulbs in foil.

3. Wash beet, leaving it whole, and wrap it in foil. Add the foil-wrapped garlic bulbs and beet to the baking dish. Roast the vegetables for 45–60 minutes at 350°F.

4. When vegetables are done, remove from oven. Scoop out the squash flesh and place it in a large stockpot along with the onion. Squeeze out the garlic flesh and add it to the pot. Add the vegetable stock. Bring the soup to a boil and then decrease the heat to low. Purée soup and season to taste with salt and pepper.

5. Peel the beet and chop into several pieces. In a food processor, blend the chopped beet and sour cream together. Add milk if necessary for a thick paste consistency.

6. Serve the soup with a spoonful of beet mixture delicately feathered out with a bread knife to give a star shape.

The nutty roasted garlic flavour stands out. The star effect with the beet mixture makes an appealing presentation.

Pesto Squash Soup   Serves 6–8

5 cups chopped squash or pumpkin, or 3 cups cooked and mashed
4 cups chicken stock
2 tablespoons butter
2 garlic cloves, chopped
3 large onions, chopped
1 red pepper, chopped
1/2 teaspoon nutmeg
1/4–1/2 teaspoon cumin
pinch of ginger
salt and pepper to taste
1 cup whipping cream or milk
1/2 cup packed fresh parsley
1/2 cup packed fresh basil
1 large garlic clove
1/4 cup olive oil

1. In a large saucepan, add squash and chicken stock. Cook covered for approximately 10 minutes or until just tender. Set aside.

2. In another saucepan, melt butter over medium heat. Sauté the chopped garlic, onion and red pepper, stirring for 3–5 minutes or until softened. Stir in the squash mixture. Add nutmeg, cumin, ginger, salt and pepper and bring to a boil. Reduce heat and simmer, partially covered, stirring occasionally for 20 minutes.

3. Purée squash mixture until smooth, using a hand blender or food processor.

4. Stir in whipping cream and cook until heated through. Taste and adjust seasonings if required.

For pesto, blend the parsley, basil, garlic clove and olive oil together in food processor. Swirl a generous tablespoonful into each bowl of soup.

Dilled Squash Soup   Serves 4–6

3 cups acorn or butternut squash, peeled and cut into 1" cubes
2 apples, peeled, cored and quartered
1 large onion, chopped
4 cups chicken or vegetable broth
2 teaspoons dried dill weed
1/2 teaspoon dried thyme
1/2 teaspoon salt
2 cups milk, broth or water

1. In a large saucepan, combine squash with all ingredients except milk. Cover and bring to a boil. Reduce the heat and simmer covered, stirring occasionally, until squash is tender, approximately 35 minutes.
2. Purée mixture, using hand blender or food processor.
3. Stir in milk, and heat over medium-low until heated through.

• • •

Chickpea and Spinach Soup with Garlic   Serves 4

1 can chickpeas (540 ml or 19 oz.), rinsed and drained
3 cups chicken broth
8 garlic cloves, peeled and left whole
1 1/2 teaspoons dried oregano
1/4 teaspoon dried rosemary
2 cups packed fresh spinach, chopped coarsely

1. In a saucepan over medium-high heat, add chickpeas, broth, garlic, oregano and rosemary, and bring to a boil. Reduce heat to low and simmer for approximately 10 minutes, stirring occasionally.
2. Purée mixture until smooth.
3. Stir in spinach. Cover and cook over medium heat for 5–7 minutes.
4. Serve immediately.

Carrot and Chive Soup   Serves 4

2 tablespoons butter or vegetable oil
1 medium onion, sliced
2 garlic cloves, chopped
3 cups carrots, peeled and sliced
2 tablespoons flour
5 cups chicken or vegetable stock
1/2 cup light cream or milk
1/4 cup chopped fresh chives
salt and pepper to taste

1. Heat butter or oil in a saucepan over medium heat. Sauté onion, garlic and carrots until vegetables are slightly softened, approximately 5 minutes. Mix in flour.

2. Slowly pour in stock while stirring. Bring to a boil and simmer until carrots are tender, approximately 30 minutes.

3. Purée soup and stir in cream or milk and chives, retaining some chives for garnish when serving.

4. Bring to a boil once again and simmer until ready to serve.

A nice, bright orange soup with green flecks.

French Onion Soup with Garlic   Serves 6

1 tablespoon butter
2 tablespoons olive oil
4 large onions, thinly sliced
4 garlic cloves, finely chopped
1 teaspoon sugar
1/2 teaspoon dried thyme
2 tablespoons flour
8 cups chicken or beef stock
1 loaf French bread, thickly sliced and toasted
1 garlic clove, halved
3 cups grated Swiss cheese

1. In a saucepan, cook onions over medium heat with butter and olive oil for 10–12 minutes or until onions are just beginning to brown. Add the garlic, sugar and thyme, and continue to cook for 30–35 minutes, stirring occasionally, until onions are well browned.

2. Add flour and stir until well blended.

3. Gradually add the stock. Bring to a boil. Reduce heat and continue to simmer for approximately 30 minutes, skimming off the foam from time to time.

4. Preheat broiler. Rub each slice of bread with the cut ends of the garlic clove. Fill 6 ovenproof soup bowls 3/4 full. Float one or two slices of bread over the soup and sprinkle with grated cheese.

5. Broil for 3–4 minutes or until cheese begins to bubble.

Exquisite!

Baked Onion Soup   Serves 4–6

6 large onions, sliced
1 whole garlic bulb, peeled and chopped
3 cups chicken stock
2 tablespoons butter
1/2 teaspoon thyme, dried
1 teaspoon salt
1/4 teaspoon pepper
2 cups chicken stock
1 cup milk or cream

1. Place onions, garlic, 3 cups of stock, butter, thyme, salt and pepper in a casserole. Cover and bake at 350°F for one hour.

2. Remove onion soup from oven. Purée mixture, using a hand blender.

3. Add 2 cups of chicken stock and milk or cream. Continue to bake for 10–15 minutes or until heated through.

4. Serve garnished with parsley.

A thick soup that boasts a rich flavour.

Chicken Soup with Garlic   Serves 8

1 medium onion, cut in half widthwise
1 whole chicken (1–1.3 kg or 2–3 lb)
2 carrots, peeled and cut into quarters
3 stalks celery, cut into quarters
2 parsnips, peeled and cut into quarters
1 whole garlic bulb, separated into unpeeled cloves
1 bay leaf
10–12 cups water
1/4 cup parsley, chopped
salt and pepper to taste

1. Heat stove element to medium-high and place cut side of onion directly onto hot element. Cook onion until cut side is blackened, approximately 2–3 minutes. Set aside.

2. Wash chicken in cold water and add to large stockpot with carrots, celery, parsnips, garlic and bay leaf, including the charred onion, using enough water to cover.

3. Bring to a boil and skim off the foam floating on top of soup. (Removing the foam will give you a nice clear soup.) Continue to cook over low heat until chicken is cooked, approximately 1 hour. Remove chicken, bay leaf and garlic from stock and continue to simmer. Discard bay leaf. If soup will be eaten that day, skim off fat floating on top and discard.

4. From the cooked garlic cloves, squeeze out the garlic pulp and mash it with a few tablespoons of stock. Return garlic to stockpot .

5. When chicken is cool enough to handle, break it into bite-size pieces and return to pot. (You may not want to add all the meat to the soup. Store leftover meat for other dishes.)

6. Serve with fresh parsley sprinkled on top.

In the winter, if you want to make your winter birds happy, keep your chicken skin and blend it in food processor until smooth. Shape and freeze into a rectangular shape to fit into a suet holder or simply spread directly onto fir tree branches. They will love you for it!

Clear Garlic Soup   Serves 4–6

1 cup olive oil
1 teaspoon salt
8 garlic cloves, peeled and left whole
1 bay leaf
dash black pepper
dash thyme
dash sage
8–9 cups water
1/4 cup chopped parsley
toasted croutons (optional)

1. Place all ingredients in a pot, except parsley and croutons. Boil for 5–7 minutes. Garlic should be soft.

2. When ready to serve, strain through a flour sieve.

3. Serve with toasted croutons and a sprinkling of chopped parsley.

A very elegant soup and a great alternative for a meat-based consommé. Yes, the olive oil quantity is correct.

Quick Chickpea Soup   Serves 4

    1 tablespoon olive oil
    1 medium onion, chopped
    2 garlic cloves, finely chopped
    1/2 teaspoon dried basil or Italian herbs
    2 tablespoons tomato paste
    5 cups chicken or vegetable stock
    3/4 cup small pasta shapes, such as shells
    1 can chickpeas (540 ml or 19 oz.), rinsed and drained
    salt and pepper to taste
    grated Parmesan cheese

1. In saucepan, heat oil over medium heat. Add onion, garlic and basil.
   Cook, stirring, for approximately 2 minutes or until softened. Add
   tomato paste. Stir.

2. Add stock to onion mixture. Bring to a boil.

3. Stir in pasta and chickpeas. Partially cover and cook, stirring
   occasionally, for 8–10 minutes or until pasta is tender.

4. Season with salt and pepper. Serve with Parmesan cheese.

You may substitute other types of canned beans or lentils for the
chickpeas in this recipe.

Variation: For a chickpea and spinach soup, increase stock to 6 cups and
stir in 4 cups of chopped spinach or Swiss chard along with chickpeas and
pasta.

Lentil and Squash Soup   Serves 8

8 cups chicken or vegetable stock
3/4 cup green lentils, sorted, rinsed and drained
1 1/2 cups squash, peeled and shredded or chopped
2 carrots, peeled and chopped
1 stalk celery, chopped
1 large onion, chopped
3 garlic cloves, chopped
1 teaspoon dried thyme or marjoram
1/4 cup fresh dill or parsley, chopped
salt and pepper to taste

In a large stockpot, combine the stock, lentils, squash, carrots, celery, onion, garlic and thyme. Bring to a boil. Reduce heat. Cover and simmer for 35–40 minutes or until lentils are tender. Stir in dill or parsley.

So easy—toss it in the pot and your stove does the work!

• • •

Garlic Potato Soup   Serves 5

4 cups chicken or vegetable stock
3 medium potatoes, peeled and diced
20 garlic cloves, peeled and left whole
1 1/2 cups milk
2 tablespoons butter
1 1/2 teaspoons fresh rosemary, finely chopped,
    or 1/2 teaspoon dried and crumbled
salt and pepper to taste

1. In a saucepan, bring to a boil the stock, potatoes and garlic. Reduce heat to medium and continue to cook for approximately 15 minutes or until potatoes and garlic are tender.

2. Purée soup and stir in the milk, butter and rosemary.

3. Season with salt and pepper. Continue to cook until heated through.

This soup may be prepared the day before.

Vegetable Barley Soup   Serves 8

    2 tablespoons butter
    1 large onion, chopped
    3 garlic cloves, chopped
    1 1/2 cups turnip, peeled and diced
    1 1/2 cups squash, peeled and diced
    1/2 teaspoon dried thyme or marjoram
    8 cups chicken or vegetable stock
    1/2 cup pearl barley, rinsed
    salt and pepper to taste

1. In a saucepan over medium heat, sauté the onions and garlic in butter for a few minutes. Add turnip, squash and thyme or marjoram. Cook, stirring often, until vegetables are light coloured, approximately 5 minutes.

2. Stir in stock and barley and bring to a boil. Decrease heat and simmer for approximately 30 minutes or until barley is tender.

3. Season with salt and pepper.

A delicious, hearty soup. You may substitute other vegetables, including carrots, potato, parsnip or cauliflower, for the turnip in this recipe.

Split Pea Pumpkin Soup   Serves 10

2/3 cup yellow split peas, soaked overnight (see below)
8 cups chicken stock
3 cups pumpkin, peeled and cubed
1 large onion, chopped
2 slices bacon, fried and crumbled
1 teaspoon mixed herbs, such as thyme, marjoram or oregano
1/4 cup fresh parsley, chopped
salt and pepper to taste

1. Pick through the split peas and then rinse in cold water. Place split peas in a large bowl and cover with water to soak overnight.

2. Drain peas and discard water. In a large stockpot, add the peas, stock, pumpkin, onion, bacon and mixed herbs. Bring to a boil for approximately 20 minutes. Reduce to low and simmer until the pumpkin and peas are tender, approximately 1 1/2 hours.

3. Purée in a blender or food processor along with the parsley.

A quicker method, allowing for same-day use of the split peas, is to boil the peas in plenty of water (approximately 4 cups) for several minutes. Remove from heat and let soak approximately 1 hour. Drain. Return to stockpot along with the rest of the ingredients and cook in same manner over medium-low heat until just tender.

Homemade Soup from Leftovers

Serves 4–6

1–2 tablespoons butter or oil
1/4 cup chopped onion or 1–2 cloves chopped garlic
4–5 cups stock
2 cups any combination of the following:
    fresh vegetables, chopped
    cooked vegetables, chopped
    uncooked pasta, rice, barley
    cooked pasta or rice
    leftover meats, beans, cold cuts
1 tablespoon fresh herbs of your choice, chopped,
    or 1 teaspoon dried
salt and pepper to taste
3/4 cup milk or cream (optional)

1. In a large stockpot, sauté the onion and/or garlic in butter or oil.

2. Add stock, along with 2 cups of your choice of soup additions and herbs. Bring to a boil and reduce to simmer until the soup is cooked and heated through.

3. Soup may be served as it is, or puréed and enriched with 3/4 cup of milk.

Soups are a wonderful way to "hide" leftovers and create unique and delicious recipes at the same time!

Vegetables

Cooking Squash

To Bake:
Cut squash in half lengthwise and scoop out seeds and stringy pulp. Place cut side down in a shallow baking dish in approximately 1" of water. Bake at 375°F for 45–60 minutes or until tender. Can be eaten quartered, stuffed or with flesh scooped out and mashed.

For Hubbard squash: After baking, turn cut side up and dot with butter, maple syrup and pepper. Bake for an additional 10 minutes.

For spaghetti squash: Bake whole at 375°F for 50–60 minutes. Slice in half lengthwise and scoop out seeds and stringy fibre. Using fork, scrape strands from the outer shell. If all the strands do not come away, bake a little longer. Toss with tomato sauce, olive oil and herbs and serve with Parmesan and green onions. Makes a great low-calorie pasta-like dish.

For turban squash: Bake whole at 375°F for 50–60 minutes. Slice in half, or try serving it in its own shell by slicing off the top third. Discard seeds. Scoop out the flesh and mash and stir with chopped green onions and butter. Season with salt and pepper.

To Microwave:
a)   Cut squash in quarters, removing seeds. Place in a large casserole with 1/2 cup water. Microwave on High for 15–20 minutes, or until tender when pierced with fork. Let stand 15 minutes or until cool enough to handle. Eat whole or mashed.

b)   Pierce whole squash in several places with a sharp knife. Microwave on High for 8–12 minutes for small-size squash (allow approximately 6–7 minutes per pound of squash) or until tender when pierced with knife. Turn squash over partway through cooking time.

When cooked, let stand approximately 10 minutes or until cool enough to handle. Cut in half, remove seeds, scoop out flesh and mash.

To Steam:

Cut squash into pieces (removing seeds and stringy pulp) and steam cut side down until tender, approximately 25 to 35 minutes. Scoop out flesh and mash.

To Boil:

Peel and cut squash into pieces with seeds and stringy pulp removed. Cover with water and boil until tender, approximately 15 to 20 minutes.

To Roast:

Peel and seed squash and cut into chunks. Place in a shallow baking dish and sprinkle with olive oil and salt. Bake at 400°F for 30 minutes or until tender and nicely browned.

To Barbecue:

Cut squash in half lengthwise, scoop out seeds and stringy pulp, and dot cavity with butter. Place squash halves back together and wrap in foil. Grill over barbecue for 20–30 minutes, turning over several times during cooking. Season with salt, pepper, herbs and spices as desired.

Suggested Squash Seasonings:

- butter and maple syrup or honey with salt and pepper;

- grated orange rind, orange juice, pinch of ginger, with salt and pepper;

- applesauce with pinch of cinnamon and nutmeg.

Tips:

To cut and peel squash, cut off the stem and base with a chef's knife. Remove the peel with a vegetable peeler.

For squash with deep ridges, such as acorn squash, cut squash into thick rings and peel the rings.

Pumpkin and squash can be interchanged in most recipes.

To make squash easier to slice, make a small slit in the squash with a knife and microwave it on High for approximately 2 minutes.

Squash Gratin   Serves 6–8

3–4 garlic cloves, chopped
2 tablespoons flour
1/2 teaspoon dried summer savory or crumbled marjoram
1 teaspoon coarse salt
pepper to taste
6 cups squash, such as butternut, peeled, seeded and diced
2 tablespoons olive oil

1. In a small bowl, combine garlic, flour, summer savory, salt and pepper.

2. In a greased baking dish, coat the squash well with the flour mixture. Drizzle coated squash with olive oil and toss again.

3. Bake covered at 400°F for approximately 20 minutes. Uncover and continue to bake for another 20 minutes or so or until lightly browned.

• • •

Roasted Pumpkin with Brown Sugar and Garlic Glaze
Serves 4–6

4 cups pumpkin, peeled and cut into 1" cubes
1/2 cup butter, melted
1/2 cup brown sugar
2 garlic cloves, chopped
1/2 teaspoon pepper

1. Place pumpkin cubes in a 9" x 12" roasting pan. Drizzle melted butter over pumpkin cubes. Sprinkle brown sugar, garlic and pepper over pumpkin cubes and stir to coat.

2. Bake at 375°F for approximately 30 minutes or until pumpkin is cooked through and lightly browned.

Squash Galette   Serves 4-6

4 cups squash, such as butternut, peeled, seeded and diced
2-3 garlic cloves, chopped
2 tablespoons vegetable or olive oil
1 teaspoon black pepper
1/2 teaspoon salt
1 1/2 cups onion, thinly sliced
1 tablespoon vegetable or olive oil

1. Place squash in baking dish in a single layer. Sprinkle with garlic, 2 tablespoons oil, pepper and salt. Toss well to coat. Bake uncovered at 350°F for approximately 25 minutes or until tender, turning occasionally.

2. Meanwhile in frying pan, cook onion slowly with 1 tablespoon oil for approximately 20 minutes until onion is a deep golden brown.

3. Mix cooked onion with cooked squash and press mixture firmly into an ungreased shallow pan (can use the same dish used to bake the squash). Cover with foil and bake for 30 minutes or until heated through.

4. Invert the squash mixture onto a serving platter and serve.

Cinnamon Roasted Squash   Serves 4

      2 small acorn squash or one large squash
      2 tablespoons butter, melted
      2 tablespoons honey
      1 teaspoon cinnamon
      pinch nutmeg
      1/2 teaspoon coarse salt
      pepper to taste

1. Cut squash in half through the stem. Using a soup spoon, remove the seeds and stringy fibre. Cut in wedges 1–2" thick and arrange skin side down in a shallow roasting pan.

2. In a small dish, combine butter, honey, cinnamon, nutmeg, salt and pepper.

3. Brush squash with honey/butter mixture and bake at 400°F for 35–40 minutes or until squash is tender and golden brown.

Squash is both tasty and attractive when cut in wedges.

Squash with Caramelized Onions   Serves 4–6

4 large onions
1 tablespoon butter
4 cups squash, peeled and diced into 1/2" cubes
3 tablespoons sugar
1 teaspoon coarse salt
1/4 teaspoon pepper
1 tablespoon balsamic vinegar

1. Cut onions in half, and then into half moons, 1/2" thick.

2. In a large frying pan over medium-high heat, cook onions in butter until soft, approximately 15 minutes.

3. Add squash, sugar, salt and pepper. Continue to cook, uncovered, for approximately 45 minutes, stirring occasionally, until onions are very soft and light brown in colour. If pan dries, add water a tablespoon at a time.

4. Stir in balsamic vinegar and keep warm until ready to serve.

You may choose to omit the vinegar, as this dish tastes equally delicious without it.

• • •

Maple Squash Baked   Serves 4

1 medium squash, cut in half horizontally and seeded
2 tablespoons maple syrup
1 tablespoon butter

Place squash cut side up in a shallow baking dish. Dot cavity of squash with butter and sprinkle with maple syrup. Cover lightly with foil. Bake at 375° F for 40 minutes or until tender.

Maple Squash Mashed   Serves 4

    1 medium squash, peeled, seeded and cut into large chunks
    2 tablespoons maple syrup
    1 tablespoon butter
    salt and pepper to taste

Boil squash until tender, approximately 20 minutes. Drain and mash. Add
maple syrup and butter. Season with salt and pepper.

• • •

Curried Squash   Serves 4

    1 small acorn or butternut squash, peeled,
        seeded and cut into large chunks
    1 onion, chopped
    1 garlic clove, crushed
    1 tablespoon butter or vegetable oil
    1/2 teaspoon curry powder
    1/2 teaspoon cumin
    salt and pepper to taste

1. Boil squash for 20 minutes or until tender. Drain, reserving a little
   vegetable water.

2. Meanwhile, sauté onion and garlic in butter or vegetable oil for 2–4
   minutes or until onion is tender. Stir in curry powder, cumin, salt and
   pepper.

3. Add onion mixture to cooked squash and mash, seasoning further
   to taste. Heat through.

Ginger Squash Rings   Serves 4

1 small acorn squash (1/2 kg or 1 lb.)
3 tablespoons honey
1 tablespoon soy sauce
2 teaspoons vinegar, rice or white
1 1/2 teaspoons fresh ginger, peeled and minced
2 garlic cloves, chopped

1. Cut off both ends of the squash. Cut squash crosswise into 4 rings, approximately 3/4" thick. Scoop out seeds and discard.

2. Place squash rings in single layer onto a greased baking sheet. Cover with foil and bake in 400°F oven until squash begins to soften, approximately 15 minutes.

3. Meanwhile, whisk honey, soy sauce, vinegar, ginger and garlic in a small bowl.

4. Remove foil from squash, and brush half of honey mixture over the squash rings. Sprinkle with salt and pepper. Bake uncovered at 400°F for 10 minutes.

5. Remove squash from oven, turn over and brush on the remaining honey mixture. Continue to bake until squash is brown, tender and glazed, an additional 10 minutes or so.

Barbecue Squash Rings   Serves 4

    1 medium acorn squash
    1/4 cup olive oil or melted butter
    1-2 garlic cloves, chopped
    1 teaspoon dried herbs such as rosemary or oregano

1. Slice squash into 1/2" rounds. Remove seeds and stringy fibre.
   (To make it easier to slice, make a small slit in the squash and
   microwave it on High for approximately 2 minutes.)

2. Mix together the olive oil or butter, garlic and herbs.

3. Place squash on vegetable barbecue tray, and brush with garlic
   mixture. Grill with lid down until squash is tender, approximately
   10 minutes, turning over occasionally.

It is best to barbecue the squash rounds using a vegetable/fish grilling
tray, as they are easier to handle and less likely to fall through the larger
slits of the barbecue rack.

• • •

Stir-Fry Spinach   Serves 4

    1 tablespoon olive oil
    6 garlic cloves, thinly sliced
    1 package spinach (284 g or 10 oz.), washed, with stems removed
    1 tablespoon soy sauce
    1/4-1/2 teaspoon pepper

Heat skillet or wok over medium-high heat. Add oil and garlic, stirring
constantly for approximately 2 minutes or until garlic begins to brown.
Add spinach and cook for 2-3 minutes, stirring constantly, until spinach
is wilted and hot. Add soy sauce and pepper, and stir to mix well. Serve
immediately.

Even those not too fond of spinach will say, "Not bad, not bad at all!"

Glazed Barbecue Squash   Serves 4

    1 medium acorn squash
    1/4 cup brown sugar
    1/2 teaspoon cinnamon
    dash nutmeg
    2 tablespoons butter
    salt and pepper to taste
    pecans, chopped (optional)

1. Cut squash in half lengthwise. Discard seeds and stringy pulp.

2. In a small bowl, mix together brown sugar, cinnamon and nutmeg. Generously sprinkle each squash half with the sugar mixture and dot with 1 tablespoon of butter. Wrap each half tightly in foil.

3. Grill on barbecue over low heat for 25–30 minutes or bake in a 350°F oven for 30–40 minutes or until tender.

For even tastier squash, sprinkle cooked squash with toasted pecans and broil for a few minutes or until sugar is bubbly.

• • •

Pan-Fried Garlic Potatoes   Serves 4

    2 tablespoons butter
    4–5 medium potatoes, peeled and cubed to 1/2"
    3–4 garlic cloves, coarsely chopped
    1/2 teaspoon salt or to taste

1. In a frying pan, melt butter over medium-high heat. Add potatoes, garlic and salt.

2. Cook, uncovered, turning occasionally, until potatoes are tender and nicely browned.

To cook faster, cover with lid. The potatoes will not be as crispy on the edges, but they will be just as delicious.

Potatoes in Garlic Sauce   Serves 4

4 medium potatoes, peeled and quartered
1 egg
2 garlic cloves, finely chopped
1/2 teaspoon salt
1/4 teaspoon dry mustard
1/8 teaspoon pepper
1/8 teaspoon curry powder, optional
2 tablespoons vinegar
1/2 cup vegetable or olive oil

1. Boil potatoes for 10 minutes until tender. Drain. Cover and keep warm.

2. Prepare sauce by beating together egg, garlic, salt, mustard, pepper, curry powder and 1 tablespoon vinegar. Add 1/4 cup oil, a small amount at a time, beating or whisking after each addition. Slowly, beat in remaining vinegar and oil.

3. Pour sauce over hot cooked potatoes and serve. Any remaining sauce may be stored in the refrigerator for up to 3 days.

Try this with diced squash, too.

Garlic Roast Potatoes with Rosemary   Serves 6

5–6 large potatoes cut into 1 1/2" chunks
10–12 garlic cloves, unpeeled
1/4 cup olive oil
2 teaspoons dried rosemary or 2–3 sprigs fresh
salt and pepper to taste

In a shallow baking dish, large enough to accommodate potatoes in a single layer, toss potatoes with garlic, olive oil, rosemary, salt and pepper. Bake at 400°F for 50–60 minutes, turning potatoes occasionally, until crisp and golden brown.

The garlic may be eaten too! Squeeze out the pulp and try it with a bite of potato, or on bread.

A great dish to serve when entertaining.

• • •

Garlic Mashed Potatoes   Serves 6

6 medium potatoes, peeled and quartered
6 garlic cloves, peeled and left whole
1 tablespoon olive oil
1/2 teaspoon pepper
salt to taste

1. Place potatoes and garlic cloves in pot and cover with cold, salted water. Bring to a boil and cook until potatoes are tender, approximately 25 minutes.

2. Drain potatoes and garlic but reserve cooking liquid. Mash potatoes and garlic, slowly adding olive oil and some of the cooking liquid until potatoes reach desired consistency.

3. Season to taste with pepper and salt.

Garlic Baked Potatoes   Serves 3

    3 large baking potatoes, washed and scrubbed
    1 whole garlic bulb (approximately 6 cloves)
    1 tablespoon olive oil
    1/4 cup chicken broth
    1/4 cup sour cream
    3 tablespoons grated cheddar or cheese of choice
    dash paprika
    freshly ground pepper to taste

1. Pierce the potatoes in several places with a fork. Place potatoes directly on oven rack and bake at 425° F until soft, approximately 50 minutes.

2. Meanwhile, slice through the tops of the garlic cloves exposing some garlic flesh. Place cloves on a piece of foil, 6" square.

3. Sprinkle cloves with olive oil. Wrap and bake at 425°F until cloves are soft, approximately 20 minutes.

4. Allow potatoes and garlic to cool.

5. Slice off approximately 1/4 from the lengthwise top of each potato. Using a spoon, scoop the potato pulp into a bowl, leaving the skin intact. Squeeze the garlic flesh into the bowl of potato pulp and mash slightly.

6. Add the broth, sour cream and pepper, and mix lightly.

7. Spoon the mixture into the potato skins. Sprinkle with cheese and paprika.

8. Place potatoes on a baking sheet and bake at 425°F for approximately 15 minutes or until browned and heated through.

Potatoes and garlic may be placed in oven at the same time—check cooking times for each.

Milk and salt may be used as a substitute for chicken broth and sour cream in this recipe.

Onion and Garlic Mashed Potatoes

Serves 4–6

 1 tablespoon margarine or butter
 2 garlic cloves, chopped fine
 1 cup onion, chopped
 5–6 medium potatoes, peeled and quartered
 1/2 cup chicken stock
 1/3 cup sour cream
 1/4 teaspoon pepper

1. Melt butter or margarine in a frying pan over medium heat. Sauté garlic and onions for approximately 4 minutes or until softened. Set aside.

2. Boil potatoes in water until tender, approximately 20 minutes. Mash potatoes with chicken stock, sour cream and pepper.

3. Add onion and garlic mixture to the mashed potatoes. Stir well and serve.

• • •

Straw Mat Potatoes

Serves 4

 4 medium potatoes
 3 garlic cloves, chopped
 salt and pepper to taste
 4 tablespoons butter (or a mixture of butter and olive oil)

1. Peel and grate potatoes, and rinse well in cold water. Drain and wrap in tea towel to dry. Transfer potatoes to a bowl along with garlic and salt and pepper. Mix well.

2. Heat butter over medium-high heat until smoking hot in frying pan. Press in potato mixture to make a 1/2" layer. Cook uncovered for 10 minutes or until crisp on bottom. Turn over and cook for another 5 minutes or so.

A unique presentation!

Oven-Roasted Vegetables   Serves 6

5 cups of any combination of the following, cut into 3/4 " pieces:
  potato, squash, turnip, onion, sweet potato, carrot or parsnip
2-3 tablespoons olive oil
1/2 teaspoon salt
1/2 teaspoon sugar
pepper to taste
1 tablespoon dried rosemary or 1 sprig fresh
2-3 cloves garlic, chopped
2-3 tablespoons balsamic vinegar or lemon juice

1. Place vegetables in a single layer in shallow baking dish.

2. Mix all seasonings together, including vinegar, in a small bowl and pour over the vegetables. Stir well to coat.

3. Bake at 400°F for 30-45 minutes or until vegetables are tender, stirring occasionally.

This dish will always be very tasty, no matter what vegetable combination is chosen.

Stir-Fry Vegetables with Feta Cheese   Serves 4

1 small eggplant
3 sweet peppers, red, green and/or yellow
1 medium red onion
1 1/2 cups mushrooms, halved
2 tablespoons balsamic vinegar
2 tablespoons olive oil
1 teaspoon Dijon mustard
4 garlic cloves, chopped
2 tablespoons fresh thyme or basil or 1 teaspoon dried
1/2 cup feta cheese, crumbled

1. Cut up eggplant, peppers and onion into 1" pieces. In a large bowl, toss cut vegetables with mushrooms, balsamic vinegar, olive oil, Dijon, garlic and thyme or basil.

2. Stir-fry in a frying pan on medium-high heat for approximately 20 minutes or barbecue in a grill basket or tray.

3. Before serving, stir in feta cheese.

Green Beans with Garlic

Serves 4

 3 cups green beans, trimmed and cut into 2" pieces
 1 small onion, chopped
 3 garlic cloves, chopped
 2 tablespoons butter
 1 can tomato sauce (approximately 200 ml or 7.5 oz.)
 1 teaspoon pepper
 1 teaspoon oregano, dried
 salt to taste

1. Cook beans in a small amount of water until tender crisp, approximately 6–8 minutes. Drain.

2. Meanwhile, sauté the onion and garlic in butter in a small frying pan for approximately 3 minutes. Add tomato sauce and seasonings. Cook a few minutes more.

3. Add the beans and toss well with tomato sauce mixture. Heat through.

• • •

Carrots with Garlic

Serves 4

 7–8 medium carrots, sliced into 1/4" rounds
 4 garlic cloves, peeled and sliced
 2 tablespoons butter
 salt and pepper to taste

1. In a medium saucepan, cook carrots and garlic in a little water until just done, approximately 6–8 minutes. Add butter, salt and pepper. Stir.

2. Remove cover and cook until all the liquid has evaporated and carrots have taken on a nice glaze.

Try this with other vegetables, too!

Stir-Fry Broccoli
Serves 4

1 large bunch broccoli
2 teaspoons olive oil
2 garlic cloves, crushed
3/4 cup chicken broth or water
pinch salt and pepper
2 tablespoons freshly grated Parmesan cheese

1. Cut broccoli florets into bite-size pieces. Slice broccoli stalks into 1/4" rounds. Keep stalks and florets separate.

2. Heat oil, garlic, broth and seasonings in saucepan over medium-high heat. Add stalk pieces and cook, stirring often, until approximately 1/2 the liquid has evaporated and the stalks are almost tender, approximately 3 minutes.

3. Toss in florets and increase heat to high. Stir-fry until florets are bright green in colour, approximately 4–5 minutes.

4. Sprinkle with Parmesan cheese and serve.

Meat and Fish

Garlic Chicken

Serves 4–6

4 chicken halves (skin removed, if preferred)
2 whole garlic bulbs, broken up but unpeeled
4 carrots, peeled and sliced into 1" pieces
3 potatoes, peeled and cut into quarters or sixths
1 teaspoon dried rosemary
3/4 cup water
salt and pepper to taste

1. Season chicken halves on both sides with a generous pinch of salt and pepper. Arrange in a shallow roasting pan. Place garlic in one corner of pan (cloves will be easier to remove later if kept all together). Arrange carrots and potatoes around chicken, and sprinkle chicken and vegetables with rosemary.

2. Roast at 375°F, uncovered, basting occasionally, until juices run clear when chicken is pierced with a knife.

3. Set garlic cloves aside.

4. Transfer chicken and vegetables to a serving platter. Cover.

5. To make sauce, discard fat from pan and transfer sauce and 3/4 cup water to a small saucepan. Scrape off any browned bits from pan with a little hot water, and add to the saucepan. Bring sauce to a boil over medium heat.

6. Meanwhile, squeeze garlic cloves from their skins and add to sauce, mashing garlic as it is stirred.

7. Season sauce with salt and pepper, and serve with chicken.

Saté (Satay) Chicken   Serves 4

4 chicken breasts, skinned and boned
3 tablespoons soy sauce
2 tablespoons lemon juice
4 garlic cloves, chopped
1/4 teaspoon cayenne
3 garlic cloves, peeled and left whole
1 small onion, or 3 green onions
1 cup roasted unsalted peanuts
1–2 hot peppers
1–2 tablespoons fresh ginger, grated
1 tablespoon soy sauce
2 tablespoons brown sugar
juice of 1/2 lemon
1 cup water
1–2 tablespoons vegetable oil

1. Cut chicken into thin strips. Mix together in a bowl: 3 tablespoons of soy sauce, 2 tablespoons lemon juice, chopped garlic and cayenne. In a covered container, marinate the chicken pieces with this mixture for approximately 2 hours in the refrigerator.

2. For saté sauce: In food processor, mix together 3 cloves of garlic, onion, peanuts, hot pepper, ginger, 1 tablespoon soy sauce, brown sugar, lemon juice and water. Transfer to a double boiler and simmer for approximately 30 minutes, stirring occasionally.

3. In a wok or frying pan, heat the vegetable oil on high heat. Stir-fry the marinated chicken for 5–7 minutes or until chicken is cooked through.

4. Serve chicken and sauce with rice and/or tender-crisp vegetables.

This also makes a great barbecue chicken dish. Simply cut the chicken into 3/4" chunks and marinate as indicated. Skewer the chicken pieces. Brush with 2 tablespoons of vegetable oil and cook for approximately 10 minutes on the barbecue. Serve with the saté sauce.

Sweet and Sour Chicken   Serves 6

6 chicken breast halves, boned and skinned
  or 1 whole chicken, cut in pieces
1 egg, beaten and placed in separate bowl
1/4 cup cornstarch
cooking oil
3/4 cup sugar
4 tablespoons ketchup
1/2 cup vinegar
1 tablespoon soy sauce
2 garlic cloves, chopped

1. Dip chicken breasts in the beaten egg and then roll in the cornstarch.

2. In a small amount of oil, fry the chicken until just browned. Place in a shallow baking dish.

3. Mix together sugar, ketchup, soy sauce and garlic, and pour over chicken.

4. Bake uncovered at 325°F for approximately 1 hour, turning the chicken every 15 minutes or so.

Children love this!

Baked Ginger Chicken   Serves 4

1/4 cup vegetable oil
1/2 teaspoon pepper
3 garlic cloves, chopped
1/8 teaspoon thyme
1/8 teaspoon basil
1 1/2 tablespoons freshly-grated gingerroot or 1 teaspoon dried
4 chicken breasts
paprika

1. In a large bowl, mix together the oil, pepper, garlic, thyme, basil and ginger. Drop in the chicken pieces and stir to coat.

2. Arrange chicken snugly in a shallow baking dish, skin side up, pouring any excess sauce over the chicken. Sprinkle with paprika.

3. Bake at 350°F for 35–40 minutes or until chicken is tender.

Couscous with Chicken   Serves 4

1 cup quick-cooking couscous
1 tablespoon olive oil
1 cup boiling water
1 teaspoon olive oil
2 sweet peppers, red or yellow, cut into thin strips
1/2 cup chopped green onions (red onion may be substituted)
3 garlic cloves, chopped
4 skinless, boneless chicken breast halves
1/2 cup chicken broth
1 medium tomato, chopped
1/2 cup dried apricots and/or prunes, chopped
1 teaspoon chili powder
3/4 teaspoon ground coriander
1/4 teaspoon ground cloves
1/4 teaspoon ground ginger
2 teaspoons lemon juice

1. In a medium bowl, mix couscous with 1 tablespoon of olive oil until well coated. Add boiling water. Let stand approximately 5 minutes and stir with fork. Set aside.

2. In frying pan over medium heat, stir-fry peppers, green onions and garlic in 1 teaspoon olive oil until vegetables are crisp-tender.

3. Add chicken and brown each side for approximately 4 minutes. Stir in the broth, tomato and dried apricots or prunes. Cook for several minutes and add the chili powder, coriander, cloves and ginger. Cook until chicken is no longer pink in the centre, approximately 5–7 minutes. Stir in the lemon juice.

4. Serve chicken and sauce on a bed of fluffed couscous.

The dried fruit complements the chicken in this recipe.

Chicken with Lemon Herb Marinade   Serves 6

juice of 1 lemon
2 teaspoons oregano
1/4 cup fresh parsley, chopped
1 teaspoon salt
1/4 teaspoon pepper
2 garlic cloves, chopped
1 small onion, finely chopped
1 teaspoon hot chilies, chopped
1/3 cup cooking oil
3 large chicken breasts, split and boned

1. Combine all marinade ingredients in a small bowl.

2. Place chicken in a container or a plastic bag. Add marinade. Marinate, covered, in the refrigerator for at least 2 hours, turning occasionally.

3. Barbecue or broil chicken pieces for 6–8 minutes on each side, depending on thickness.

Chicken with Lemon and Rosemary Marinade   Serves 4

1/3 cup olive oil

1 teaspoon salt

1/2 teaspoon pepper

pinch crushed chili peppers

2–3 garlic cloves, chopped

2 tablespoons fresh rosemary, chopped or 1 teaspoon dried, crushed

3 tablespoons lemon juice

1 teaspoon grated lemon peel

4 chicken breasts, skinned, boned and thinly sliced

1. In a small bowl, mix together marinade ingredients. Toss with sliced chicken. Marinate for approximately 1 hour, covered, in the refrigerator.

2. Stir-fry in wok or frying pan on high heat.

Serve with rice and stir-fried vegetables.

For a change, substitute pork tenderloin, veal chops or lamb for the chicken in this recipe. The marinade may also be used with fish or seafood, but marinate pieces no longer than 10 minutes or the lemon juice will "cook" the fish.

Barbecue Chicken Marinade   Serves 4

1/2 cup green onions, chopped
1/2 cup tomato sauce
1/4 cup teriyaki sauce
1/4 cup spicy mustard
1 tablespoon + 1 teaspoon cider vinegar
2 teaspoons brown sugar, firmly packed
2 teaspoons molasses
2 garlic cloves, chopped
1 1/4 lbs chicken breasts (approximately 1/2 kg), skinned and boned
parsley sprigs for garnish

1. In a large bowl, mix together all ingredients except chicken and parsley. Add chicken and coat well with the marinade. Cover and chill for 1 hour, turning chicken after approximately 30 minutes.

2. Barbecue chicken, turning several times and basting with marinade, until chicken is tender and juices flow clear when chicken is pierced with a fork. Serve garnished with parsley.

It is best to brush barbecue rack with oil to prevent chicken from sticking.

Hearty Beef Stew   Serves 6–8

2 lbs lean stewing beef (approximately 1 kg), cut into 1" cubes
1/2 cup flour
2 tablespoons vegetable oil
2 large onions, thinly sliced
2 cups sliced mushrooms
2 garlic cloves, chopped
1 tablespoon tomato paste
2 cups beef broth
2 cups sliced carrots
2 cups squash, peeled, seeded and sliced
2 potatoes, thinly sliced
1 cup chopped celery

1. Coat beef with flour. Shake off excess flour. In a large pot or Dutch oven, brown beef in 1 tablespoon of oil over medium-high heat.

2. In a skillet, sauté onions and mushrooms in 1 tablespoon of oil until softened. Add garlic and cook, stirring, for approximately 1 minute. Transfer onion mixture to pot or Dutch oven. Add tomato paste, broth and enough water to just cover. Cover, bring to a boil and then reduce heat to low. Simmer about 1 1/4 hours or until beef is tender.

3. Add carrots, squash, potatoes and celery for last 30 minutes of cooking time.

Pumpkin Sloppy Joes Serves 4

1 lb ground beef (454 g)
1 medium onion, finely chopped
1/2 cup ketchup
1/2 cup tomato juice
1/2 teaspoon chili powder
1/2 teaspoon salt
dash ground nutmeg
dash ground cloves
1/4 teaspoon ground pepper
1 cup cooked pumpkin or squash, mashed
hamburger buns

1. In a large skillet over medium heat, cook beef and onion until meat is no longer pink. Drain.
2. Add ketchup, tomato juice, chili powder, salt, nutmeg, cloves and pepper to meat mixture. Mix well and bring to a boil. Stir in pumpkin.
3. Decrease heat, cover and simmer for 15–20 minutes.
4. Spoon mixture into buns and serve.

For an extra-special treat, use Butternut Squash Dinner Rolls (page 127).

Beef with Lemon Herb Marinade   Serves 2–4

1/4 cup lemon juice
1 tablespoon vegetable oil
2 teaspoons dried parsley
1 teaspoon dried marjoram or oregano
1 teaspoon dried thyme
1 bay leaf, crumbled
1 small onion, minced
2 garlic cloves, minced
freshly ground pepper
1 lb sirloin steak (approximately 1/2 kg)

1. Mix all marinade ingredients together. Marinate steak overnight in a covered container, turning occasionally.

2. Drain meat well, reserving the marinade.

3. Barbecue or broil the steak, brushing meat with marinade during cooking.

Perfect also for roasts. Use this marinade also as a flavour enhancer and meat tenderizer, especially with less expensive cuts of meat. Lemon juice makes the meat more tender.

Souvlaki   Serves 2–4

    1/4 cup olive oil
    3 tablespoons balsamic vinegar
    1 tablespoon fresh rosemary (or 1 1/2 teaspoons dried)
    2–4 garlic cloves, chopped
    1 teaspoon salt
    pepper to taste
    1 lb beef or chicken cubes or strips (approximately 454 g)
    3 cups mixed, cubed vegetables, such as sweet peppers,
        onions, mushrooms and zucchini

1. Mix together all marinade ingredients. Marinate chicken or beef pieces
   for at least 3 hours or overnight.

2. Skewer meat, alternating with vegetables. Grill on barbecue over
   medium-low heat for 8–12 minutes, turning and basting often with
   leftover marinade.

When using wooden skewers, it is best to soak the skewers in water for
approximately 30 minutes before skewering your meats and vegetables.
This prevents the wooden skewer from burning before the food is ready.

Garlic Pork Chops   Serves 4

4 pork chops, trimmed of visible fat
1 tablespoon butter
1/4 cup chopped onion
2–3 garlic cloves, chopped
1/2 cup long grain rice
1 1/2 cups chicken broth
1 green pepper, sliced
1 tomato, sliced
salt and pepper to taste

1. Melt butter in a frying pan and brown pork chops on each side. Remove and set aside onto a plate.

2. Using the same frying pan, lightly brown the onion and garlic for approximately 5 minutes, adding the rice for the final few minutes. Add chicken broth and stir.

3. Place pork chops over the rice and broth mixture, followed by green pepper and tomato slices. Bring broth to a steady rolling boil over medium heat. Cover and let cook for approximately 20 minutes.

4. Remove cover and cook for a further 10 minutes or so until most of the liquid has evaporated.

You may substitute 3 tablespoons of tomato paste for the tomato in this recipe and spread it over the pork chops.

Onion Apple Pork Chops   Serves 4

2 large onions
2 large apples
1 tablespoon vegetable oil
4 pork chops
1/3 cup raisins
1/2 cup apple juice
2 tablespoons brown sugar
1 tablespoon lemon juice
3/4 teaspoon cinnamon
1/2 teaspoon dry mustard
1/8 teaspoon allspice

1. Peel onions, and peel and core apples. Slice thinly and spread half the onion and apple slices in an 8" baking dish. Set aside.

2. Heat oil over high heat in a frying pan and brown chops. Place chops on onions and apples in baking dish. Cover with raisins and remaining onions and apples.

3. Drain fat from frying pan. Pour in apple juice. Add sugar, lemon juice, cinnamon, mustard and allspice. Bring to a boil and pour over chops.

4. Cover with foil and bake in 350°F oven, basting often with juices, for about 1 hour or until chops are very tender.

• • •

Rosemary Pork Tenderloin   Serves 4

4 garlic cloves, chopped
3/4 teaspoon dried rosemary or 3 sprigs fresh
3/4 teaspoon black pepper
1/2 teaspoon salt
1 tablespoon olive oil
1 to 1 1/2 lb pork tenderloin roast (500–750 g)

1. In a small dish, mix together garlic, rosemary, olive oil, black pepper and salt. Rub the mixture over roast.

2. Place roast in a shallow baking pan. Roast for approximately 30 minutes at 400°F or until centre is no longer pink when cut with a knife.

This dish smells heavenly!

Pork Saté (Satay)   Serves 4–6

1/4 cup butter
1 tablespoon lemon juice
1 tablespoon grated lemon rind
1/2 teaspoon Tabasco sauce
3 tablespoons grated onion
3 teaspoons brown sugar
1 teaspoon coriander
1/2 teaspoon ground cumin
1/4 teaspoon ginger
1 to 2 garlic cloves, chopped
1/2 cup teriyaki or soy sauce
1 1/2 lbs pork tenderloin (approximately 750 g),
    cut into 3/4" cubes
3 cups mixed, cubed vegetables, such as onions,
    sweet peppers and zucchini

1. In saucepan, melt butter over low heat and add lemon juice, lemon rind, Tabasco sauce, onion, brown sugar, coriander, cumin, ginger, garlic and teriyaki sauce. Simmer for 5 minutes. Marinate pork in sauce overnight in a covered container in the refrigerator.

2. Skewer the meat, alternating with vegetables, and grill on barbecue for approximately 15 minutes, basting and turning every few minutes.

If using wooden skewers, it is best to soak them in water for approximately 30 minutes before skewering to prevent sticks from burning.

Prepare extra sauce to pour over a side dish of rice!

Garlic Salmon on the Barbecue   Serves 4

5 large garlic cloves, peeled and left whole
1/2 cup vegetable oil
1/4 cup water
1/4 cup soy sauce
1 teaspoon Worcestershire sauce
1 tablespoon fresh parsley, chopped fine
1 teaspoon salt
1/2 teaspoon pepper
dash cayenne pepper
4 salmon fillets, approximately 250 g or 1/2 lb each

1. Boil garlic in a small saucepan, with just enough water to cover garlic, for approximately 5 minutes. Remove from heat and drain. Transfer garlic to a small dish and mash with a fork.

2. In a mixing bowl, combine all marinade ingredients, including the crushed garlic. Add salmon fillets and turn to coat well with the marinade. Marinate for 30 minutes at room temperature or 1 hour in the refrigerator.

3. Grill the salmon on the barbecue, basting every few minutes with the marinade. Salmon is ready when flesh flakes easily.

Chicken or other types of fish may be substituted; however, cooking time will have to be adjusted accordingly.

Casseroles and Main Dishes

Squash and Bean Stew

Serves 6

1 tablespoon olive oil
1 large onion, chopped
2 garlic cloves, finely chopped
1 tablespoon chili powder
1 1/2 teaspoons ground cumin
1 can tomatoes (796 ml or 28 oz.), diced
3 cups butternut squash, peeled, seeded and cut into 1" cubes
1 1/2 cups green beans, trimmed, cut into 1" pieces
1 can black beans (540 ml or 19 oz.), rinsed and drained
1 tablespoon jalapeño, seeded and finely chopped
1/2 cup chopped fresh coriander (cilantro)
salt and pepper

1. Heat oil in a large pot over medium heat. Add onion and sauté until tender and golden, approximately 7 minutes.

2. Add garlic, chili powder and cumin. Continue to cook for approximately 1 minute.

3. Add tomatoes and bring to a boil. Stir in squash and green beans.

4. Reduce heat. Cover and simmer until vegetables are almost tender, approximately 12 minutes.

5. Stir in black beans and jalapeño, and cook approximately 5 minutes longer. Stir in coriander. Season with salt and pepper to taste.

Fall Vegetable Stew   Serves 6

2 tablespoons butter or vegetable oil
1 onion, cut into 1/2" wedges
4 garlic cloves, chopped
1 carrot, thickly sliced
1 1/2 cups squash or pumpkin, peeled and cut into 1/2" cubes
1 1/2 cups turnip, peeled and cut unto 1/2" cubes
1 teaspoon dill
1 teaspoon thyme
1 teaspoon pepper
1 teaspoon salt
3 cups stock, water or cider
2 green peppers, coarsely chopped
6 tomatoes, chopped
1 cup corn kernels (canned or frozen)
1 1/2 cups broccoli or cauliflower
1 1/2 cups cooked chicken (optional)

1. Heat butter or oil in a large pot over medium-high heat. Add onions and garlic and sauté for a few minutes. Stir in carrots, squash and turnip. When coated with hot oil, add dill, thyme, pepper and salt. Add stock.

2. Bring mixture to a boil and add remaining vegetables and chicken. Cover and cook on medium-low until vegetables are tender.

Serve with thick slices of crusty bread.

Eggplant Stew
Serves 4–6

1 cup onion, chopped
3 garlic cloves, chopped
1 tablespoon olive oil
1 medium eggplant, peeled and diced
1 1/2 cups squash, peeled, seeded and shredded
1 large red or green pepper, diced
2 cups chopped tomatoes
1 tablespoon fresh basil leaves, chopped, or 1 teaspoon dried
2 tablespoons white vinegar
salt and pepper to taste
hot pepper sauce (optional)

1. In a large saucepan over medium heat, sauté onion and garlic in olive oil until soft, approximately 5 minutes. Stir in eggplant, squash, red or green pepper, tomatoes, basil and vinegar.

2. Bring mixture to a boil. Lower heat and simmer gently for 20 minutes, or until vegetables are soft and mixture has thickened. Add salt, pepper and hot pepper sauce to taste.

• • •

Roasted Ham, Potato and Pumpkin Dinner
Serves 4

2 cups cooked ham, cut into 3/4" cubes
4 cups potatoes, cut into 3/4" cubes
2 cups pumpkin, peeled and cut into 3/4" cubes
1/2 cup melted butter
3 garlic cloves, chopped
2 teaspoons salt
1/2 teaspoon pepper

Combine all ingredients in a shallow 9" x 12" roasting pan. Bake at 350°F for approximately 45 minutes or until vegetables are cooked through and slightly browned.

Cooked sausage cut into 3/4" pieces may be substituted for the ham in this recipe.

Squash and Onion Casserole   Serves 4–6

3 cups squash, peeled and diced to 1/4" or 1/2" size
1 cup celery, diced
1 cup onion, diced
1/2 cup butter
1 1/2 cups boiling water
1 1/2 cups cracker crumbs
2 eggs, beaten
1 cup grated cheese
salt and pepper to taste
wheat germ or crushed cereal for topping

1. In medium saucepan, partially cook vegetables with butter and water for approximately 5 minutes.

2. Transfer cooked vegetables and liquid to a casserole dish. Stir in cracker crumbs, eggs and cheese. Season with salt and pepper. Top with wheat germ or crushed cereal.

3. Bake at 350°F, uncovered, for 30–40 minutes.

This dish can be made a day ahead and stored in the refrigerator. Leftovers may be frozen, but this dish is so tasty that leftovers are unlikely!

Stuffed Pumpkin .   Serves 6

1 pie pumpkin (approximately 8"–9" in diameter)
1 1/2 lbs ground beef (approximately 750 g)
1 medium onion, chopped
1/2 cup fresh mushrooms, sliced
1 can condensed cream of mushroom soup (284 ml or 10 oz.)
3 tablespoons soy sauce
2 tablespoons brown sugar
1 1/2 cups cooked rice
vegetable oil

1. Wash pumpkin. Cut off a cap from the top of the pumpkin, approximately 6" round. Set cap aside. Remove seeds and loose fibre from the inside. Use a metal spoon to do the final cleaning.

2. In a frying pan over medium heat, cook ground beef with onion and mushrooms until meat is no longer pink. Drain and return mixture to pan.

3. To meat mixture, add soup, soy sauce and brown sugar. Simmer for approximately 10 minutes. Stir in rice.

4. Spoon beef mixture into pumpkin and replace pumpkin cap. Place stuffed pumpkin into a greased pan, rubbing oil over the outside of pumpkin as well. Bake in a 350°F oven for 1 to 1 1/2 hours or until pumpkin is tender.

5. Serve dish directly from the pumpkin, scooping out some pumpkin flesh along with the meat mixture.

This is an ideal recipe for fall when pumpkins are plentiful. Do not discard the pumpkin seeds. Try roasting them. You could also use this "pumpkin pot" idea with your favorite chili recipe.

Baked Vegetable Stew   Serves 6–8

1 medium eggplant, peeled and cut into 1" cubes
2 large potatoes, peeled and cut into 1" cubes
2 large green peppers, cut into 1" chunks
1 large Spanish or red onion, finely chopped
2 large tomatoes
2 cups squash, peeled and cut into 1" cubes
5 garlic cloves, chopped
2 tablespoons olive oil
2 teaspoons dried basil
1 teaspoon oregano
1 teaspoon salt
1/2 teaspoon pepper
1/2 teaspoon cayenne pepper
1 tablespoon sugar
2 tablespoons balsamic vinegar
1/2 cup chopped fresh basil, oregano or parsley as topping
1 garlic clove, chopped
grated peel of 1 lemon

1. Place all vegetables into a deep casserole (at least 3-litre or 12-cup size).

2. In a small bowl, stir together garlic, oil, basil, oregano, salt, pepper and cayenne. Add to casserole and mix with vegetables until evenly coated.

3. Bake, uncovered, for approximately 1 1/2 hours at 375°F, stirring at least every half hour. (Baking uncovered allows some juices to evaporate. If the vegetables are drying up too fast, the dish may be covered.)

4. Remove from oven. Sprinkle with sugar and vinegar, and stir until well mixed. Add additional salt, sugar or vinegar to taste.

5. Just before serving, sprinkle with 1/2 cup chopped parsley, chopped garlic clove and grated lemon peel.

This is a great side dish for entertaining. It can be eaten hot, cold or at room temperature. Freezes well.

Pumpkin Risotto

Serves 4

1/4 cup butter
1/3 cup red onion, chopped
2 garlic cloves, chopped
1 1/4 cups uncooked Arborio rice
2 1/4 cups hot vegetable stock
3 cups pumpkin, peeled and chopped or shredded
or 2 cups cooked and mashed pumpkin
1/4 cup grated Parmesan cheese
1 tablespoon fresh basil, chopped, or 1 teaspoon dried
1 to 2 tablespoons chopped toasted pecans* (optional)

1. Melt butter in a large saucepan. Add onions and garlic, and cook over medium-low heat for 2 minutes, or until soft. Stir in the uncooked rice for approximately 1 minute, or until well coated.

2. Add 1/2 cup of stock, stirring constantly until all the liquid is absorbed. Add pumpkin and stir. Continue adding more stock, approximately 1/2 cup at a time, stirring constantly, for 25 minutes, or until all the stock is absorbed and the rice is tender and creamy in texture.

3. Stir in the Parmesan cheese and basil. Serve topped with pecans.

* To toast pecans: Place nuts in small pan over low heat and stir constantly until light brown in colour. Watch carefully—once the nuts begin to brown, they burn very quickly.

The pumpkin risotto has a most appealing golden yellow colour.

Bacon and Herb Risotto

Serves 4–6

1/3 cup olive oil
1 large red onion, cut into thin wedges
1/2 lb sliced bacon (approximately 200 g), cut into small pieces
2 garlic cloves, chopped
2 cups uncooked Arborio rice
2 teaspoons fresh rosemary, chopped, or 3/4 teaspoon dried
4 tablespoons fresh chives cut into 1" lengths
6 cups hot chicken or vegetable stock
2 teaspoons fresh basil, chopped, or 3/4 teaspoon dried

1. In a large saucepan over medium heat, sauté onion in olive oil for approximately 5 minutes. Add half the chopped bacon and continue to cook until bacon is just crisp.

2. Stir in garlic, rice, rosemary and half the chives, and cook for 1 to 2 minutes, or until well coated.

3. Add 1/2 cup of hot stock, stirring constantly over medium heat until all the stock is absorbed. Continue adding more stock, approximately 1/2 cup at a time, stirring constantly, for 25 minutes, or until the stock is absorbed.

4. Meanwhile, broil the remaining bacon until crisp. Drain on paper towels. (A toaster oven is ideal for broiling small quantities.)

5. Stir basil and remaining chives into the risotto. Adjust seasonings. Garnish with the crispy bacon and additional chives.

Wild Rice and Squash   Serves 5–6

1 cup wild rice
2 1/2 cups boiling water
1 1/2 cups fresh mushrooms, sliced
1 1/2 cups squash, peeled and cubed
2 medium onions, finely chopped
1/2 cup green pepper, chopped
3 garlic cloves, chopped
2 tablespoons olive oil
1/2 cup chicken broth
1 tablespoon soy sauce
1/2 teaspoon dried savory
1/4 cup toasted sliced almonds* (optional)

1. Rinse rice. Drain. In medium pot, combine rice with boiling water. Bring to a boil, uncovered, and reduce heat to simmer. Cover and simmer for 35–40 minutes, or until all water has been absorbed.

2. In a large frying pan, sauté mushrooms, squash, onions, green pepper and garlic in olive oil for a few minutes, or until vegetables are crisp-tender. Stir in the cooked rice.

3. Add broth, soy sauce and savory. Cover and simmer for 10–15 minutes, or until squash is tender.

4. Toss with almonds, if desired.

* To toast almonds: Place almonds in a small frying pan over medium heat, stirring frequently, until nuts take on a golden colour. Watch carefully—once the nuts begin to brown, they burn very quickly.

Spaghetti Squash with Vegetables   Serves 4-6

1 to 2 lb spaghetti squash
1 tablespoon margarine or olive oil
3/4 cup chopped onions
3 garlic cloves, finely chopped
1 1/2 cups sliced mushrooms
3/4 cup chopped green or red pepper
1 cup tomato sauce
1 teaspoon dried oregano
1 teaspoon dried basil
1/4 cup grated cheese of choice

1. Pierce squash in several places. Microwave on High for 8-10 minutes or until soft. Cool and slice lengthwise in half. Discard seeds. Scrape out strands with a fork. If cooked enough, strands will lift out easily.

2. Meanwhile, in a large skillet, heat oil or melt margarine. Sauté onions, garlic, mushrooms and peppers for approximately 5 minutes.

3. Add spaghetti squash strands and cook for approximately 2 minutes.

4. Add tomato sauce, oregano and basil. Combine well.

5. Pour mixture into a baking dish and sprinkle with cheese. Broil for 2 minutes or until cheese is browned.

Coconut Ginger Squash Casserole   Serves 4

  2 cups cooked and mashed butternut squash
  2 large eggs, beaten
  1/2 cup milk
  2 1/2 tablespoons butter or margarine, melted
  2 tablespoons shredded coconut
  1 teaspoon vanilla
  1/2 teaspoon ground ginger
  2 teaspoons sugar

In a large bowl, thoroughly mix together all ingredients. Transfer to a lightly greased casserole dish and bake uncovered at 350°F for 50–60 minutes.

• • •

Onion and Apple Casserole   Serves 4–5

  6 medium onions
  4 medium apples
  3 tablespoons flour
  2 tablespoons sugar
  1 teaspoon salt
  1 1/2 tablespoons butter

1. Peel and slice onions thinly.

2. Wash, core and slice apples. Mix together flour, sugar and salt. Toss with sliced apples.

3. Alternate apples and onions in layers in a greased baking dish. Dot with butter. Cover and bake in 350°F oven for 30 minutes or until tender. Uncover to brown top, if desired.

Serve as a side dish with roast pork or pork chops. A must to try in the fall!

Polenta with Squash and Red Pepper   Serves 4

2 2/3 cups chicken broth
1/8 teaspoon salt
2/3 cup cornmeal
2 teaspoons olive oil
1 medium onion, thinly sliced
2 garlic cloves, chopped
2 teaspoons sugar
1 red pepper, sliced
1 1/2 cups squash, peeled and shredded
4 tablespoons balsamic vinegar
4 tablespoons fresh basil, chopped, or 2 teaspoons dried
2/3 cup feta cheese, crumbled

1. Heat chicken broth and salt in saucepan until boiling. Slowly add cornmeal, stirring constantly until mixture becomes very thick. Remove from heat and place into a lightly greased 13 1/2" x 11" baking dish, spreading out so that mixture covers the bottom of the dish. Set dish aside.

2. In a medium frying pan, sauté onion and garlic in olive oil until onions are soft, approximately 5 minutes. Sprinkle with sugar and continue to cook until onions are golden, approximately 5 minutes more. Add pepper and squash, and cook for 10 minutes or until vegetables are soft. Stir in the vinegar, basil, and feta cheese.

3. Lay pepper and squash mixture over the cornmeal. Bake at 350°F for 15 minutes or until heated through.

An attractive side dish to enhance any meal. You may not have known that cornmeal could taste so good!

Cabbage Roll Casserole   Serves 4–6

1 1/2 lb ground beef (approximately 750 g)
2 medium onions, chopped
1 to 2 garlic cloves, minced
1 teaspoon salt
1/4 teaspoon pepper
1 can tomato sauce (398 ml or 14 oz.)
1 cup water
1/2 cup uncooked long grain rice
4 cups shredded cabbage
sour cream (optional)

1. In a large frying pan, brown beef, onions and garlic until meat is no longer pink. Drain.

2. Add salt and pepper, tomato sauce and water. Bring to a boil and stir in rice. Cover and simmer for approximately 20 minutes.

3. Place half the shredded cabbage in a greased baking dish. Cover with half the rice mixture. Repeat.

4. Cover and bake for 1 hour at 350°F.

5. Serve with sour cream, if desired.

Stuffed Pizza   Serves 6

3 teaspoons sugar
approximately 3 1/4 cups flour
3 teaspoons salt
4 tablespoons vegetable oil or olive oil
2 tablespoons quick-rising yeast
1 1/4 cups warm water
1 can tomatoes (796 ml or 28 oz.), drained and crushed
2 tablespoons olive oil
1 teaspoon oregano, dried or 1 1/2 tablespoons fresh chopped
2 teaspoons basil, dried or 3 tablespoons fresh, chopped
2 garlic cloves, chopped
1/4 cup grated Parmesan cheese
1 bag fresh spinach (284 g or 10 oz.), rinsed, coarsely chopped
2/3 cup mozzarella cheese, grated

1. Mix sugar, flour, salt, oil and yeast in food processor, adding water gradually through feeder tube. Let food processor run approximately 1 to 2 minutes until dough forms one clump. Remove dough. It will be sticky. Knead with a little more flour by hand and let rise in greased bowl, covered, for approximately 1 hour or until doubled in size.

2. In medium bowl, mix tomatoes, 2 tablespoons of olive oil, oregano, basil, garlic and Parmesan cheese. Set aside.

3. In another bowl, toss spinach with grated mozzarella cheese and set aside.

4. Grease two 9" cake pans with oil.

5. Punch down dough when risen. Cut in half. Take each half and cut dough into a 1/3 and a 2/3 piece.

Stuffed Pizza, *continued*

6. Roll out each larger piece so that it will cover the bottom of cake pan and slightly overlap the edges. In each cake pan, place 1/2 of the spinach filling. The volume of filling will decrease as pizza bakes. Roll out remaining pieces of dough to a 9" diameter size. Place on top of pan with spinach mixture. Fold over edges of top and bottom dough to seal. Spread 1/2 of sauce over the top of each pizza. Slit dough in a few places on top.

7. Bake at 450°F on lower rack for 10 minutes. Transfer the pans to the upper rack in oven and continue to bake at 450°F for another 30 minutes.

For variety, you may knead some herbs, chili flakes, grated cheese or crushed garlic into the dough. To give your crust added texture, sprinkle some cornmeal onto the pan before adding rolled dough.

Garlic Waffles with Chicken and Sauce

Yield: approximately 7 waffles (6" in diameter) and 2 1/3 cups sauce

1/4 cup butter
2 garlic cloves, chopped
1 1/2 cups flour
2 tablespoons sugar
3 teaspoons baking powder
1/2 teaspoon salt
2 eggs, beaten
1 1/2 cups milk
4 tablespoons butter
5 tablespoons flour
3/4 teaspoon salt
1 3/4 cups milk
1 cup cooked chicken or turkey, chopped

1. In a small pan, melt butter and sauté garlic for a few minutes over medium-low heat. Set aside.

2. Mix together flour, sugar, baking powder and 1/2 teaspoon salt.

3. In a separate bowl, mix together eggs and 1 1/2 cups of milk. Stir in the garlic/butter mixture as well as the flour mixture. Beat well.

4. Pour batter onto hot waffle iron and cook until nicely browned. Keep in warm oven on platter until ready to serve.

5. Meanwhile, to make sauce, melt 4 tablespoons butter in medium saucepan over medium heat and stir in the flour and salt until smooth.

6. Add 1 3/4 cups milk, stirring continuously with whisk until sauce thickens, approximately 10 minutes. Stir in the chicken and heat through.

7. Serve waffles with white sauce and your choice of vegetable or salad.

Try these waffles with your other favourite toppings.

Pasta

Pasta Tips

1. Recommended servings per person:
   For side dish—90 g or 3 oz.
   For main course—120–150 g or 4–5 oz.
   With spaghetti, a 25-cent-diameter bunch will serve one person.

2. Pasta should be cooked, uncovered, in a large pot of boiling salted water. This water should be at a good rolling boil when the salt is added to the water. The timing for cooking begins from the time water has returned to a boil after adding pasta.

3. Do not add oil to the cooking water as pasta will not adhere to the sauce.

4. Al dente means pasta is ready when it has a slight bite to it, that is, is not soft. The package times are only guidelines; you may have to remove a noodle occasionally to verify.

5. Cooked pasta should not be rinsed, as it removes the starch that allows the pasta to stick to the sauce. For cold pasta salad, however, the pasta is rinsed.

6. If using pasta in a baked dish, only half cook the pasta as it will continue to cook in the oven.

7. You may cook pasta ahead of time if you wish. Cook pasta al dente. Drain. To reheat, drop into boiling water for 30–60 seconds. Drain and serve.

8. Chunky sauces go better with chunky pasta shapes, while lighter, smoother sauces go best with long, thin pasta.

Pasta Tips, *continued*

9. Always serve more pasta than sauce.

10. The best pasta is made from 100% durum wheat flour or semolina which comes from Italy. The colour should be that of straw; too yellow a colour means that food colouring has most likely been added. The surface finish should be dull as opposed to shiny. Shiny pasta has been dried too quickly which impacts on the flavour and its ability to hold the sauce. The best surface texture is one that is slightly rough. You will see this more in the handmade brands.

Basic Tomato Sauce   Serves 4

 3 tablespoons olive oil
 3 garlic cloves, coarsely chopped
 1 medium onion, chopped
 1 can whole plum tomatoes (796 ml or 28 oz.)
 1 teaspoon sugar
 salt and pepper to taste
 2 tablespoons olive oil

1. In medium pan over medium-low heat, sauté garlic and onion with olive oil until garlic is lightly golden and/or onion is translucent.

2. Drain tomatoes, removing seeds if desired. Chop or crush tomatoes and add to pan along with sugar and seasonings. (You may place undrained tomatoes in pan. Sauce will be more liquid, but with longer cooking time the sauce will thicken as the liquid evaporates.) Cook until the sauce thickens, approximately 10–15 minutes.

If desired, add a little more olive oil to the sauce so that there is a film of oil on the surface. This helps the sauce to adhere to the pasta.

This sauce is simply delicious on its own when served with your choice of pasta and sprinkled with freshly grated Parmesan cheese. It also makes a great base for the addition of other herbs, cooked meats, vegetables and cheeses, and is wonderful as a pizza sauce.

Linguini with Fresh Tomato Sauce   Serves 4–6

    5 medium tomatoes, chopped
    1/4 cup green onions, chopped
    1/3 cup fresh basil, chopped
    2 garlic cloves, chopped
    1/4 teaspoon black pepper
    2 tablespoons balsamic vinegar
    1 tablespoon olive oil
    1 package linguini pasta (450 g)
    grated Parmesan cheese

1. Place tomatoes, green onions, basil, garlic and pepper in a large bowl and toss well.

2. Mix vinegar and oil in a small dish. Add to tomato mixture. Cover and let sit at room temperature for approximately 20 minutes, stirring occasionally.

3. Cook pasta according to package directions. Drain. Pour tomato mixture over pasta and serve immediately with freshly grated Parmesan cheese.

A good summer meal when tomatoes are plentiful and tasty. To make this meal even more substantial, add real bacon bits or chopped cold cuts.

Pesto

Yield: 3 cups

2 cups firmly packed basil leaves
1/2 cup fresh parsley, chopped
3 tablespoons pine nuts
1/2 cup olive oil
2 garlic cloves, peeled and left whole
1 teaspoon salt

1. Blend all ingredients in a food processor until mixture is a thick purée, making sure sides have been scraped down into the blade of blender.
2. Spoon into a storing container or jar and pour a small amount of olive oil over pesto to prevent discolouring. Cover tightly.
3. When ready to serve, warm pesto and toss with cooked, drained pasta and freshly grated Parmesan cheese.

You may freeze pesto by placing it in ice cube trays. When frozen, remove from cube tray and store in freezer bags for use in your pesto dishes or as a flavouring for your tomato sauces, stews or meat dishes.

Spinach Pesto   Serves 4–6

1 1/2 cups fresh spinach, washed and well packed
1/4 cup water or chicken stock
3 tablespoons olive oil
2 tablespoons toasted pine nuts* (optional)
3 tablespoons grated Parmesan cheese
2 garlic cloves, chopped
salt and pepper to taste
3/4 package linguini, fettuccini or spaghetti
   (approximately 375 g)

1. In a food processor, purée spinach, water, oil, nuts, cheese, garlic, salt and pepper until smooth. Set aside.

2. Cook pasta in boiling water according to package instructions. Drain and place in a serving bowl.

3. Toss with spinach mixture and serve immediately.

* To toast pine nuts: Place pine nuts in a frying pan over medium heat for 2 to 3 minutes, stirring frequently, until they start to brown. Watch carefully as they will brown and burn quickly.

Even kids love this spinach dish!

Spinach and Feta with Pasta

Serves 6

1 bag spinach (284 g or 10 oz.)
  or 1 bunch Swiss chard (1/2 kg or 1 lb), washed
2 tablespoons olive oil
1 medium onion, finely sliced
3 garlic cloves, chopped
2 tablespoons water
2 teaspoons chopped fresh rosemary or 1 teaspoon dried
2/3 cup feta cheese, cut into cubes
salt and pepper to taste
1 package bow-tie pasta (450 g)
2 tablespoons butter

1. Chop spinach and set aside. If using Swiss chard, separate the stems and leaves and chop separately.

2. In a large frying pan over medium-high heat, sauté the onion and garlic in olive oil for approximately 2 minutes. Add the Swiss chard stems along with the water and cook for another 2 minutes.

3. Add spinach or chard leaves, rosemary and feta cheese. Cover and cook for a few minutes or until leaves have wilted. Season with salt and pepper.

4. Cook pasta in boiling salted water as per package directions. Drain. Return pasta to pot and mix with butter. Add leafy green mixture to the pasta and toss. Serve immediately.

Spaghetti with Garlic, Olive Oil and Chili Pepper   Serves 4

3/4 package spaghetti (approximately 400 g)
6 tablespoons olive oil
5 garlic cloves, peeled and left whole (or coarsely chopped
    for more garlic flavour)
1 small dried chili pepper
1/4–1/2 cup parsley, chopped (optional)
1/2 cup Parmesan cheese (freshly grated is best)

1. In a frying pan over medium heat, heat olive oil. Add garlic and chili pepper. (Chili pepper may be left whole or broken up. Breaking up the chili pepper will make the dish hotter.) Cook until garlic is golden. Remove chili pepper and discard.

2. Cook pasta in boiling salted water as directed on package.

3. Drain pasta and place in a large serving bowl. Pour flavoured hot oil over the pasta and mix well to coat all the spaghetti strands. Add chopped parsley and cheese and serve immediately.

Garlic may be left whole or chopped coarsely and either removed with the chili pepper or left in. If left in, the golden garlic takes on a wonderful nutty taste.

Spaghetti Primavera   Serves 4

1 package spaghetti (450 g)
3 carrots, sliced
4 red or green peppers, diced
3 cups bite-size pieces broccoli and/or cauliflower
1 cup squash, peeled, seeded and shredded or diced
3 tablespoons butter
5 garlic cloves, chopped
6 green onions, sliced
1 tablespoon dried basil or 1/4 cup fresh
1/4 teaspoon pepper
1 cup Parmesan cheese (freshly grated is best)

1. In saucepan, melt butter and sauté garlic, green onions, basil and pepper for a few minutes. Remove from heat and set aside.

2. Cook spaghetti according to package directions, adding carrots, red pepper, broccoli and cauliflower for last 4 minutes of cooking time. Drain.

3. In serving dish, gently toss the spaghetti-vegetable mixture with the onion mixture and cheese. Serve immediately.

Pasta with Leeks and Squash   Serves 4-6

2 leeks
4 tablespoons olive oil
2 cups squash, peeled and shredded
1 cup simmering water or chicken broth
salt and pepper to taste
1 package fusilli pasta (450 g)
1 tablespoon salt
1 to 2 teaspoons lemon peel, grated
1 to 2 tablespoons fresh parsley, chopped, or 1 teaspoon dried
freshly grated Parmesan cheese

1. Using white portion of the leek, split each leek in half and slice into thin half circles. In a frying pan over low heat, heat the olive oil and add leeks and squash. Stir until well coated with olive oil, and cook for 10-20 minutes or until softened but not browned.

2. Add water or broth and season with salt and pepper. Simmer for 10-20 minutes or until most of the liquid has evaporated.

3. Meanwhile, boil water in a large pot. When water is at a rolling boil, add 1 tablespoon salt and pasta. Cook pasta until 3/4 done. Drain but reserve approximately 1 cup of pasta water.

4. Return drained pasta to the large pot along with the leek and squash mixture. Add lemon zest and parsley and approximately 1/4 cup of the pasta water. Cook over high heat, stirring the pasta until pasta is done, approximately 5-7 minutes. Add more water if pasta is still not cooked and continue to stir.

5. Serve with grated Parmesan cheese.

Chicken and Mushroom Marinara   Serves 4

3 tablespoons olive oil
6 garlic cloves, chopped
2 cups mushrooms, sliced
1 can tomatoes (796 ml or 28 oz.), crushed
1 cup water
1/2 cup chopped fresh basil (2 teaspoons dried)
1 tablespoon dried oregano
1/4 teaspoon pepper
1/4 teaspoon salt
4 chicken breasts, skinned, boned and sliced into strips
1 package angel hair pasta such as vermicelli or other fine pasta
(approximately 500 g)

1. In a frying pan, add oil and garlic and cook over medium heat for approximately 2 minutes. Toss in mushrooms and sauté for another 2 minutes.

2. Stir in crushed tomatoes, water, basil, oregano, pepper and salt. Increase heat to high. Bring to a boil, then decrease to low and simmer, uncovered.

3. Stir chicken into sauce and continue to simmer.

4. Cook pasta according to package directions. Drain. Place pasta in a large serving dish or pot. Top with the sauce and serve immediately.

If not ready to serve immediately, keep sauce on simmer and cook pasta just before serving. If sauce is too bitter, add a teaspoon or two of sugar.

Chicken and Creamy Tomato Linguini   Serves 4-6

2 teaspoons olive oil
1 onion, chopped
1 carrot, finely chopped
2 garlic cloves, chopped
1 can plum tomatoes (796 ml or 28 oz.)
1 teaspoon dried basil or 2 tablespoons fresh, chopped
1/2 teaspoon dried oregano or 1 tablespoon fresh, chopped
pinch salt
pinch chili flakes
1 package linguini (450 g)
1 can evaporated milk (160 ml)
2 teaspoons cornstarch
2 cups cubed, cooked chicken

1. Heat oil in medium saucepan over medium heat. Add onion, carrot and garlic, and cook for approximately 3 minutes. Add tomatoes with juice, basil, oregano, salt and chili flakes. Crush tomatoes while stirring mixture. Bring to a boil, uncovered, stirring occasionally, for 10-15 minutes, or until mixture has thickened.

2. Bring a large pot of salted water to a boil. Add pasta and cook according to package directions, stirring occasionally. Drain.

3. Stir evaporated milk and cornstarch into tomato sauce. Bring to a boil, stirring occasionally, and add chicken. Cook until heated through.

4. Serve with cooked pasta.

Evaporated milk has 70% less fat than whipping cream.

Tuna Penne   Serves 6

1 tablespoon olive oil
1 onion, chopped
1 cup zucchini, diced
2 garlic cloves, chopped
2 teaspoons dried basil, or 1/4 cup fresh, chopped
1/2 bag fresh spinach (approximately 100 g), chopped
grated peel of one lemon
juice of 1 lemon
1/3 cup fresh parsley, chopped
1 package penne, rotini or fusilli (450 g)
1 can tomatoes (796 ml or 28 oz.)
1 cup crumbled feta cheese or 1 cup grated cheddar
2 cans solid white tuna (170 g or 6 oz. each, preferably
     water packed), drained

1. Heat oil in large, deep frying pan over medium heat. Add onion, zucchini, garlic and basil. Cook, stirring, for 2 minutes. Stir in spinach, lemon peel, juice and parsley.

2. Cook penne in a large pot of boiling salted water until slightly underdone (approximately 3/4 cooked). Drain.

3. Mix pasta well with the spinach mixture in frying pan. Add tomatoes, cheese and tuna until blended. Turn mixture into a large casserole dish and bake, covered, in a preheated 350°F oven for approximately 30 minutes, or until casserole is heated through.

Pasta must be slightly underdone initially, as it will continue to cook in the oven.

Pad Thai Serves 4–6

8 oz. medium-wide rice noodles (250 g)
3 tablespoons fish sauce (may substitute with soy sauce)
2 tablespoons rice vinegar or cider vinegar
2 tablespoons sugar
1 tablespoon vegetable oil
2 eggs, slightly beaten
3 garlic cloves, finely chopped
1/4 teaspoon red pepper flakes
1 cup shrimp, peeled and deveined (250 g)
1 cup tofu, sliced into thin strips
1/2 cup water
3 cups bean sprouts
6 green onions, chopped
1/2 cup fresh coriander (cilantro), coarsely chopped
1/4 cup unsalted peanuts, chopped
1 lime, cut in wedges

1. Soak noodles in hot water for 20 minutes. Drain.

2. In a small bowl, mix together fish sauce, rice vinegar and sugar. Set aside.

3. In a large frying pan or wok, heat 1 teaspoon of the oil over medium-high heat. Cook eggs, stirring, until scrambled. Cut into strips; transfer to side dish.

4. Wipe out pan and add remaining oil. Stir-fry garlic, red pepper flakes and shrimp for a few minutes. Add tofu and stir-fry for 1 minute, or until shrimp are pink and opaque.

5. Add noodles and 1/2 cup water. Cook, stirring, for 2 to 3 minutes, or until noodles are tender. Stir in fish sauce mixture, bean sprouts and half the onions; toss to mix well. Transfer to serving dish. Top with eggs, remaining onions, coriander and peanuts. Garnish with lime.

This recipe will go very quickly if all the ingredients are prepared first. Substituting chicken breast strips or beef strips for the shrimp will be just as tasty.

Breads and Desserts

Butternut Squash Dinner Rolls

Yield: 2–3 dozen rolls

2 tablespoons + 1 teaspoon active dry yeast
3/4 teaspoon + 1 cup sugar, divided
1/2 cup warm water
2 cups warm milk
1/4 cup butter or margarine, softened
2 cups squash, cooked and mashed
2 teaspoons salt
1/4 cup wheat germ
10 to 11 1/2 cups flour
1 tablespoon melted butter

1. In a large mixing bowl, dissolve yeast and 3/4 teaspoon sugar in warm water. Let stand 5 minutes, then stir down with a fork. Add milk, butter, squash, salt and remaining 1 cup of sugar. Mix until smooth. Stir in wheat germ and approximately 4 cups of flour and beat well. Add more flour until mixture forms a soft dough. Turn dough onto a floured surface.

2. Knead dough until smooth and elastic, approximately 6–8 minutes. Place in a greased bowl, turning over once to grease top of dough. Cover with a damp dish cloth and let rise in a warm place until doubled, approximately 1 hour.

3. Punch down dough and divide into thirds. Roll into a 2" sausage form and then cut into 1" pieces. Shape into balls and place on greased baking sheets approximately 2" apart. Cover and let rise until doubled, approximately 30 minutes.

4. Bake at 350°F for 15–17 minutes or until golden brown. Brush with melted butter. Cool on wire racks.

Pumpkin Puffs   Serves 4

3/4 cup flour
1 tablespoon baking powder
1/2 cup sugar
1/2 teaspoon salt
2 cups pumpkin or squash, cooked and mashed
3 eggs
1 tablespoon orange peel, finely chopped
1/2 cup sugar
1 to 2 tablespoons cinnamon
cooking oil for frying
lemon juice

1. Mix flour, baking powder, sugar and salt in a bowl. Beat in pumpkin, eggs and orange peel. Mixture should have a thick consistency. If not thick enough, add a bit more flour (may have to add more flour if using frozen cooked and mashed pumpkin).

2. In a small bowl, mix together 1/2 cup of sugar and cinnamon. Set aside.

3. Pour oil in medium pan to 1/3 full. Heat at medium-high level.

4. Drop batter into the hot oil by the teaspoonful and fry until golden, approximately 3-4 minutes, turning it over halfway to brown both sides. Drain on a paper towel. Sprinkle with sugar cinnamon mixture followed by a squeeze of lemon juice if desired.

With children around, the puffs will not have time to cool off!

Pumpkin Cinnamon Rolls   Yield: 2 dozen rolls

1 1/2 cups milk
1/4 cup sugar
1 tablespoon salt
1/4 cup shortening
1 1/2 cups pumpkin, cooked and mashed
2 teaspoons sugar
1 cup warm water
2 tablespoons active dry yeast
10 cups flour
3/4 cup butter, melted
2 1/4 cups brown sugar
3 teaspoons cinnamon

1. Heat milk with sugar, salt, shortening and pumpkin in a saucepan over medium heat or in the microwave until shortening melts, stirring occasionally. Cool to lukewarm.

2. Dissolve 2 teaspoons of sugar in warm water and sprinkle yeast over top. Let stand for 10 minutes and then stir briskly with a fork. Add yeast mixture to milk mixture along with approximately 3 cups flour. Beat until smooth. Gradually add more flour until the dough is too stiff to mix.

3. Turn dough onto a floured surface and knead for 8–10 minutes, sprinkling with more flour until dough is no longer sticky. Shape into a smooth ball and place in a large greased bowl. Cover with a damp cloth and let rise in a warm place until doubled, approximately 1 hour.

4. Meanwhile, prepare two 13" x 9" pans by generously greasing bottoms with melted butter and a sprinkling of approximately 4 tablespoons of brown sugar in each.

5. Punch down dough and divide into thirds. Roll out each third to a 13" x 8" x 1/2" rectangle. Brush each rolled rectangle with melted butter and sprinkle evenly with brown sugar and 1 teaspoon of cinnamon. Roll from the long end and slice the roll into 1" pieces. Place onto prepared pans.

6. Cover and let rise for another 45 minutes or so. Bake at 400°F for 20–25 minutes. Turn over at once and remove rolls from the pan, as the syrup will harden and the cinnamon rolls will stick to the pan.

These will not have time to cool off. They'll be gone!

Garlic and Olive Focaccia

Yield: 1 loaf

  1 tablespoon active dry yeast
  1 teaspoon sugar
  1 cup lukewarm water
  2 2/3 cups flour
  1 teaspoon salt
  3 garlic cloves, chopped fine
  1 tablespoon olive oil
  1 teaspoon rosemary, dried
  grated Parmesan cheese
  black olives, chopped, for garnish

1. Mix yeast with warm water and sugar in a small bowl. Let stand for approximately 10 minutes, then stir briskly with a fork.

2. In food processor, add flour, salt, garlic and oil. With machine running, pour yeast mixture through feeder tube slowly until dough is smooth and elastic and stays in one piece. It will be sticky.

3. Knead over counter in a small amount of flour until dough is no longer sticky. Place in a greased bowl. Cover and let rise for approximately 1 hour or until doubled in size.

4. Grease a 12" x 16" cookie sheet with olive oil.

5. Punch down dough and roll out onto a lightly floured board. Place on cookie sheet. Make depressions with thumb or fingers all over dough. Drizzle with olive oil and sprinkle with Parmesan cheese and rosemary.

6. Bake at 400°F for 25–30 minutes or until bottom of crust is browned.

7. Serve with chopped olives dropped into the depressions.

This is tasty to eat on its own, but also try it served with a 2 to 1 mixture of olive oil and balsamic vinegar as a dip.

Pumpkin Pancakes

Yield: approximately 10 pancakes (5" in diameter)

3 eggs, separated
1/4 cup brown sugar
1 cup pumpkin, cooked and mashed
3/4 teaspoon cinnamon
1/4 teaspoon ginger
dash ground cloves
1 1/2 cups flour
1 tablespoon baking powder
3/4 teaspoon salt
1 1/4 cups milk
1/4 cup butter, melted

1. Beat egg whites until stiff. Set aside.

2. Whip egg yolks until creamy and light yellow. Add brown sugar, pumpkin and spices. Stir until well mixed.

3. In a separate bowl, stir together flour, baking powder and salt. Add pumpkin mixture alternately with milk and flour mixture. Add butter. Fold in beaten egg whites.

4. Pour approximately 1/2 cup of batter onto a hot, greased frying pan or griddle. Cook until bubbles are breaking onto the surface. Flip over and continue to cook other side until lightly browned.

Serve with butter and syrup.

Pumpkin Pie

Yield: 2 pies

3 1/2 cups pumpkin, cooked and mashed
1 1/4 cups sugar
2 teaspoons ginger
1 teaspoon cinnamon
1/2 teaspoon nutmeg
pinch ground cloves
1 teaspoon salt
4 eggs, beaten
3 cups milk
2 unbaked 9" pie shells

1. Mix pumpkin, sugar and spices together.
2. Add eggs and then milk. Let mixture stand overnight in the refrigerator.
3. The following morning, fill two unbaked pie shells.
4. Bake at 350°F approximately 45 minutes or until centre of pie is set.

Make certain pumpkin is well mashed and not stringy. It is best to run it through the food processor before adding to pie mixture.

This pie filling has a nice blending of spices.

Crustless Pumpkin Pie

   3 eggs, beaten
   1/3 cup honey
   1 1/2 cups pumpkin, cooked and mashed
   1/2 teaspoon ginger
   1/2 teaspoon nutmeg
   1/2 teaspoon cinnamon
   1/4 teaspoon salt
   3/4 cup evaporated milk

1. Mix together eggs, honey, pumpkin and spices.

2. Add milk and beat until smooth.

3. Pour mixture into a deep, buttered 9" pie plate.

4. Bake at 325°F for 50–60 minutes or until centre is set when tested with a toothpick.

Chill before serving.

This recipe has all the taste of a pumpkin pie without the hassle of making a crust. The pie slices very nicely, has a custard-like texture and fewer calories, too.

Orange Pumpkin Pie

    2/3 cup brown sugar
    1 teaspoon cinnamon
    1/2 teaspoon salt
    1/2 teaspoon ginger
    1/4 teaspoon nutmeg
    1/2 teaspoon grated orange rind
    2 eggs, slightly beaten
    1 1/4 cups pumpkin, cooked and mashed
    1 cup milk
    1/3 cup orange juice, strained
    1/4 teaspoon vanilla
    1 unbaked 9" pie shell

1. Mix together brown sugar, cinnamon, salt, ginger, nutmeg and orange rind. Blend in beaten eggs.

2. Stir in pumpkin, milk, orange juice and vanilla.

3. Pour mixture into an unbaked pie shell and bake in 450°F oven for 10 minutes. Reduce heat and continue to bake at 325°F for approximately 40 minutes longer or until centre of pie is almost set.

The orange rind gives this pie a special taste.

Coconut Pumpkin Pie

1 1/4 cups pumpkin, cooked and mashed
1/2 teaspoon ginger
1/2 teaspoon cinnamon
1/2 teaspoon nutmeg
2/3 cup brown sugar
1/2 teaspoon salt
2 eggs, beaten
1 cup light cream
3/4 cup shredded coconut (toasted,* if preferred)
1 unbaked 9" pie shell

1. Mix together pumpkin, spices, eggs, cream and coconut.

2. Pour mixture into prepared pie shell and bake at 425°F for 15 minutes to lightly brown the edge of the pastry.

3. Reduce oven to 325°F and continue to bake for approximately 35–40 minutes or until filling is set at centre.

* To toast coconut: Place in a small frying pan over medium heat, stirring constantly until lightly browned.

This pie tastes even better the following day.

Pumpkin Chiffon Pie

    1 tablespoon plain gelatin (or 1 envelope)
    1/4 cup cold water
    3 eggs, separated
    1 cup sugar
    1 1/4 cups pumpkin, cooked and mashed
    1/2 cup milk
    1/2 teaspoon salt
    1/2 teaspoon nutmeg
    1/2 teaspoon cinnamon
    1/2 teaspoon ginger
    1 baked 9" pie shell

1. Stir gelatin into cold water and set aside.

2. In a double boiler, combine egg yolks, 1/2 cup of sugar, pumpkin, milk, salt, nutmeg, cinnamon and ginger. Cook, stirring constantly, until thickened. Add gelatin mixture and stir until dissolved. Remove from heat.

3. Chill until slightly thickened.

4. Meanwhile, beat egg whites until frothy. Gradually add remaining 1/2 cup of sugar, and continue beating until stiff peaks form.

5. Fold into chilled pumpkin mixture and pour into baked shell. Chill until set, at least 2 hours. Serve with whipped cream sprinkled with nutmeg or cinnamon.

This tastes very much like a traditional pumpkin pie but with a texture that is exquisite.

Pumpkin and Lime Chiffon Pie

1 tablespoon unflavoured gelatin (1 envelope)
1/4 cup cold water
1 1/2 cups pumpkin, cooked and mashed
1 teaspoon grated lime peel
1/4 cup lime juice (approximately 2 limes)
2/3 cup sugar (10 tablespoons)
3 egg whites
1/2 cup whipping cream, whipped
1 cup sliced almonds, toasted
1/2 cup whipping cream, whipped
1 baked 9" pie shell

1. Dissolve gelatin in cold water and set aside.

2. In a separate bowl, combine pumpkin, lime peel, lime juice and 4 tablespoons of sugar. Add gelatin mixture and mix well. Chill until mixture thickens somewhat.

3. Meanwhile, beat egg whites until frothy. Add remaining 6 tablespoons of sugar, 1 tablespoon at a time, beating after each addition until stiff peaks form.

4. Fold in egg whites and 1/2 cup of whipping cream (whipped) into the chilled pumpkin mixture. Pour into the baked pie shell and chill until firm, approximately 3 hours.

5. Serve with the other 1/2 cup of whipped cream (whipped) along with the toasted almonds.

You would not believe that there is pumpkin in this pie. The lime taste is thoroughly refreshing.

Pumpkin Cake with Cream Cheese Frosting

2 cups flour
2 teaspoons cinnamon
1 teaspoon baking soda
1 teaspoon baking powder
1/2 teaspoon salt
2 cups sugar
1 cup salad oil
4 eggs
1 cup pumpkin, cooked and mashed
1 cup pecans, chopped
1/2 package cream cheese (125 g), softened
1/4 cup butter, softened
1 teaspoon milk
1 teaspoon vanilla
1 3/4 to 2 cups icing sugar

1. Mix together flour, cinnamon, baking soda, baking powder and salt.

2. In a separate bowl, mix sugar, oil, eggs and pumpkin. Add the pumpkin mixture to the flour mixture. Beat well.

3. Stir in pecans and pour into a greased 9" x 13" pan. Bake at 325°F for 45–50 minutes, or until toothpick inserted in centre comes out clean.

4. For frosting: Beat together cream cheese and butter. Add milk and vanilla with gradual additions of icing sugar. Beat well until desired frosting consistency is reached.

5. Frost cake when cool.

This tastes just like a carrot cake. The nuts give it great flavour.

Bundt Pumpkin Cake   Serves 10–12

3 cups unsifted flour
2 cups sugar
4 teaspoons baking powder
2 teaspoons cinnamon
1 teaspoon nutmeg
1/4 teaspoon salt
1 cup pumpkin, cooked and mashed
1/4 cup vegetable oil
1/3 cup apple or orange juice
4 large eggs
2 teaspoons vanilla extract
1/2 cup walnuts, coarsely chopped
1/2 cup raisins
icing sugar for sprinkling

1. In a large bowl, combine flour, sugar, baking powder, cinnamon, nutmeg and salt.

2. In another bowl, beat together pumpkin, oil, juice, eggs and vanilla.

3. Stir pumpkin mixture into flour mixture until well combined. Fold in nuts and raisins.

4. Turn into a greased 10" Bundt pan and bake at 350°F for 55–60 minutes, or until toothpick inserted in centre comes out clean. Turn out of pan onto plate.

5. Sprinkle with icing sugar before serving.

Blueberry Pumpkin Muffins with Streusel Topping

Yield: 12 large or 18 small muffins

1/3 cup shortening
1 cup brown sugar, packed
1 egg
1 cup pumpkin, cooked and mashed
1/4 cup milk, evaporated milk or cream
1 2/3 cups flour
1 teaspoon baking soda
1/2 teaspoon baking powder
1/2 teaspoon salt
1 teaspoon cinnamon
1/2 teaspoon allspice
1 cup blueberries (fresh or frozen)
1 tablespoon flour + 2 tablespoons flour
2 tablespoons sugar
1/4 teaspoon cinnamon
1 tablespoon butter

1. Cream shortening and sugar in a large bowl. Add egg and beat until fluffy. Stir in pumpkin and milk.

2. In another bowl, mix flour, baking soda, baking powder, salt, cinnamon and allspice. Stir well into the pumpkin mixture.

3. Combine blueberries and 1 tablespoon flour. Gently stir into batter.

4. For streusel: Combine 2 tablespoons flour, 2 tablespoons sugar and 1/4 teaspoon cinnamon. Cut in 1 tablespoon butter until mixture is crumbly.

5. Fill paper-lined muffin tins 3/4 full and sprinkle streusel over top. Bake at 350°F for 20–25 minutes or until toothpick inserted in centre comes out clean.

Fresh, frozen or dried cranberries may be substituted for the blueberries in this recipe.

Pumpkin Cheesecake   Serves 6–8

1/2 cup crushed gingersnaps or graham crackers
1 1/2 tablespoons butter, melted
1/2 teaspoon cinnamon
1 tablespoon brown sugar
2 packages cream cheese (2 x 250 g), softened
3/4 cup sugar
3 eggs
2 tablespoons flour
1/2 teaspoon cinnamon
1/4 teaspoon ginger
1/4 teaspoon nutmeg
3/4 cup pumpkin, cooked and mashed
1 teaspoon rum flavouring

1. Combine gingersnaps, melted butter, cinnamon and brown sugar. Pat mixture firmly into the bottom of a 6 1/2 " springform pan and chill.

2. Beat cream cheese until fluffy. Gradually beat in sugar. Add eggs, one at a time, beating well after each addition. With spatula, go around edge and bottom of bowl to make certain all the cream cheese is being mixed.

3. Add flour, spices, pumpkin and rum flavouring and beat well. Pour batter over crust and bake at 325°F for 50–55 minutes, or until filling is set. Cool cheesecake first in the oven with oven turned off and door open for approximately 20 minutes and then place cake on wire rack on the counter.

4. This dessert is best refrigerated overnight before serving for flavours to blend well.

Lemon Pumpkin Cream Cheese Pie   Serves 6

1 cup graham cracker crumbs
3 tablespoons butter, melted
2 tablespoons sugar
1 package cream cheese, 250 g, softened
3/4 cup sugar
1 cup pumpkin, cooked and mashed
2 eggs
2 egg yolks
1 1/2 tablespoons flour
3/4 teaspoon grated lemon peel
1/4 teaspoon vanilla

1. For the crust: Combine graham cracker crumbs, butter and 2 tablespoons sugar. Press mixture into a 9" pie plate. Bake at 325°F for approximately 10 minutes. Remove from oven and cool.

2. Blend cream cheese and sugar. Beat in pumpkin, eggs, flour, lemon peel and vanilla until smooth.

3. Pour into cooled pie shell and bake at 350°F for approximately 35 minutes or until centre of pie is just barely firm when gently shaken. Allow the pie to cool completely in the oven with the door open.

4. Serve with a dab of whipped cream, if desired.

This pie takes on a wonderful lemony-orange colour. Very tasty with the lemon peel.

Garlic Chocolate Chip Cookies

Yield: 5 dozen

10 garlic cloves, peeled and left whole
1/2 cup liquid honey
1 cup butter
1 cup brown sugar
2 eggs
1 teaspoon vanilla
2 1/2 cups flour
1 teaspoon baking soda
1 teaspoon salt
2 cups chocolate chips
1/2 cup chopped nuts (optional)

1. Place garlic cloves in a small pot with enough boiling water to cover. Boil for 5 minutes. Drain and place garlic in a small bowl and let soak in the honey for 20 minutes.

2. Cream butter and sugar. Add eggs, one at a time, mixing well after each addition. Stir in vanilla.

3. In a large bowl, combine flour, baking soda and salt. Mix together butter and flour mixtures.

4. Using a fork, lift out the honey-soaked garlic pieces to a small plate and mash. (Do not discard the honey. This flavoured honey is great on your choice of cooked vegetable.) Add the garlic to the cookie batter and mix well. Stir in the chocolate chips and nuts.

5. Drop by heaping teaspoonfuls onto an ungreased cookie sheet. Bake at 375°F for 8–10 minutes or until lightly browned.

For a delicious variation, try this recipe with butterscotch chips instead of chocolate chips.

Garlic Shortbread   Yield: 2 dozen cookies

4 garlic cloves, peeled and halved
2 tablespoons liquid honey
1/2 cup cornstarch
1/2 cup icing sugar
1 cup flour
3/4 cup butter, softened

1. Drop garlic cloves into boiling water for 5 minutes. Drain and chop coarsely. Soak chopped garlic in honey for approximately 20 minutes. After the soaking, remove garlic pieces with a fork, draining some of the honey. Set garlic pieces aside in a small dish.

2. Sift together cornstarch, icing sugar and flour. Blend in butter and garlic pieces until a smooth dough forms. If dough is too soft to handle, chill it in the refrigerator for 20–30 minutes.

3. Roll out dough onto a lightly floured board to 1/4" thickness and cut into desired shapes. Decorate with sprinkles, candied fruit or nuts.

4. Bake at 300°F for 15–20 minutes or until edges are lightly browned. Cool on a wire rack.

As shortbread is very rich, these are nice when cut with a smaller size of cookie cutter.

They taste good, honest!

Pumpkin Swirl Cookies   Yield: 6 dozen

2 cups pumpkin, cooked and mashed
1 cup sugar
1/4 teaspoon ginger
1/4 teaspoon cinnamon
1/4 teaspoon nutmeg
1 cup chopped pecans or walnuts
1 cup shortening
2 cups sugar
3 eggs
4 cups flour
1/2 teaspoon salt
1/2 teaspoon baking soda

1. To make filling: Combine pumpkin, 1 cup of sugar and spices in a saucepan. Cook over low heat until mixture has thickened, approximately 10 minutes. Remove from heat and stir in nuts.

2. For cookie dough: Cream shortening and 2 cups of sugar until light and fluffy. Beat in eggs. Blend in flour, salt and baking soda. Dough should not be too crumbly or it will not roll well.

3. Divide dough into thirds and roll out each third onto a floured surface into a rectangle of 8" x 12". Spread 1/3 of the filling onto each dough rectangle. Starting from the long edge, roll up the dough in jelly roll fashion. Wrap in foil or plastic wrap and freeze for several hours or overnight.

4. Cut rolls to a 1/4" thickness and bake in preheated 400°F oven for 10–12 minutes or until lightly browned.

These are very attractive cookies, and are not as much work as they seem.

Frosted Pumpkin Cookies   Yield: 4 dozen

1 cup sugar
1 cup butter
1 egg
1 cup pumpkin, cooked and mashed
3 1/2 cups flour
1/2 teaspoon salt
1 teaspoon baking soda
1 teaspoon nutmeg
1 teaspoon cinnamon
1/2 cup buttermilk (or add 1 teaspoon lemon juice to
    1/2 cup milk and let stand approximately 5 minutes)
1 tablespoon butter, melted
1 tablespoon grated orange rind
1/4 cup orange juice
2 cups icing sugar, sifted

1. Cream butter and sugar. Add egg, mix well, and then add pumpkin.

2. Stir together flour, salt, baking soda, nutmeg and cinnamon.

3. Alternate additions of flour mixture and buttermilk to the pumpkin mixture until dough is no longer sticky. Chill dough for several hours.

4. Roll out dough to 1/8" thickness and cut out with desired cookie cutter shape.

5. Bake at 350°F on ungreased cookie sheets for 10–12 minutes.

6. For frosting: Mix together melted butter, orange rind and orange juice. Gradually add icing sugar, beating well after each addition, until the desired frosting consistency is reached.

Makes a very tasty cookie with an outstanding frosting.

Garlic Ice Cream   Yield: approximately 4 cups

1 1/2 teaspoons unflavoured gelatin
1/4 cup cold water
2 cups milk
1 cup sugar
1/8 teaspoon salt
2 tablespoons lemon juice
2 garlic cloves, peeled and finely chopped
2 cups whipping cream

1. In a small dish, soften gelatin in water. Set aside.

2. Heat milk over a double boiler to just simmering. Add sugar and salt and stir until dissolved. Add gelatin mixture to milk mixture. Continue to heat over medium-low heat, stirring often, for approximately 5 minutes.

3. Stir in lemon juice and garlic. Place in a container, uncovered, and chill in the freezer until slushy, approximately 2 hours.

4. Whip cream until thick but not stiff. Stir into slushy mixture. Place into a container and cover, or you may freeze the ice cream in a mould, for a few hours or overnight.

Serve with lightly sweetened fresh or canned fruit or your favourite toppings.

This ice cream is nice and creamy, just like old-fashioned ice cream but with a pleasant hint of garlic.

All About Garlic

Description

Garlic is a member of the Amaryllidacae or onion family and is one of the most common flavourings in the world, with more than 500 strains of garlic documented. There are 2 sub-species:

Hard Neck
- Large cloves with a thick central stock and colourful skins
- Skin is very easy to peel
- Generally the type that you will find locally grown
- Varieties include Porcelain (includes Music), Purple Stripe and Rocambole (includes Red Russian)
- Available from mid-July through fall
- Will keep in a cool, dry place up to spring of the following year

Soft Neck
- The most common type of garlic found in the supermarket throughout the year
- Locally grown, but not as plentiful as hard neck
- Varieties include Silverskin and Artichoke
- Skin is usually white or silvery for Silverskin, and red or purple for Artichoke
- More finicky to peel as cloves are smaller and skin finer
- Has small cloves clustered in layers within the bulb
- Easier to braid and generally stores longer than hard neck

Elephant Garlic is not really garlic, but a form of leek. One clove of elephant garlic can be as large as an entire garlic bulb. It is much milder in flavour than garlic.

Buying Garlic

Garlic should feel very firm when pressed gently in your hand. Do not buy garlic that has already sprouted, as the bulb is on its way to becoming soft, the beginning sign of deterioration. The sprout will also have a rather bitter flavour.

Storing Garlic

Small quantities of garlic, amounts that would be used within a week or so, can be stored in a kitchen cupboard away from light or moisture in containers that allow air to circulate. Do not place garlic near the kitchen sink or stove. The refrigerator is too cold and moist and causes fresh garlic to lose its flavour more quickly. Garlic must not be frozen as it will turn to mush and lose its taste. Larger quantities of garlic should be stored in a cool, dark place such as a spare, unheated room, allowing for air circulation. Garlic stored in this manner should keep from harvest time in July to the following April or May.

Planting Garlic

The actual garlic clove itself, not a seed, is used for planting. It is best to buy locally grown garlic for planting as the supermarket variety may have come from a country where the garlic may be carrying pests and diseases and may not be hardy enough for our climate. Gently break the bulb to loosen the cloves, trying not to damage or remove the skin. Plant each clove with the pointed tip up, 3"–4" deep and 6" apart, in fertile soil with good drainage. Planting in the Ottawa area, and generally throughout most of Ontario, occurs in early to mid-October, leaving time for some root formation to occur. If shoots come up before the frost, the planting was perhaps a little too early and the plant is susceptible to frost damage. After the ground has frozen, usually mid to end of November, cover the garlic with a mulch, such as straw, for winter protection as there may not be sufficient snow cover to protect it.

Unprotected garlic will most likely not sprout the following spring, as it will have frozen to a soft mush. In the spring, separate the straw from the garlic but do not remove. This will help curb weed growth and help retain moisture. If conditions are very wet in any year, the mulch may have to be removed to prevent fungus growth. For growing garlic in subsequent years, choose a different location in your garden each time.

Growing and Harvesting Garlic

Garlic needs a lot of moisture in the spring, 1" per week with decreased or no watering 3 weeks before harvest or from the 1st week of July on. When flower buds (scapes) appear on the plant, it is recommended that they be snipped or cut off so as to direct the plant energy to the growing of the bulb itself. Scapes form in early summer only on the hard neck garlic and display a curly top with a seed pod at the end that will eventually open up and flower. The scapes are wonderful to eat either fresh in salads or sauteed in butter and/or added to your favorite dish as an onion or garlic replacement. They have a mild garlic flavour. Scapes are a hot new vegetable these days, found in gourmet food sections and specialty stores. (See Garlic Scape Dip recipe on page 24).

Since freshly picked garlic scapes are only available for a short period, their use can be extended by freezing them. To do so, wash and pat dry the scapes. Chop them into 1" pieces (discarding the tips above the flower nodes). Process pieces in food processor, adding just enough extra virgin olive oil to make a light paste. Pack this paste into an ice cube tray and freeze. Store cubes in freezer bags for future use in soups, stews, stir-frys, casseroles, dips, etc.

Garlic is ready to be harvested when the bottom leaves have dried off, leaving six or so green leaves on the plant, or when 1/3 to 2/3 of the plant has dried back. It is best to loosen the soil with a spade before pulling out the garlic. Once pulled, loosen the soil from the roots as much as possible and allow the bulbs to dry on racks away from direct sunlight. Dry until the bulb wrappings are papery but stalks are still flexible, approximately a week or two. When the leaves are brown, the garlic is cured. Rub any remaining dirt off gently and store garlic until ready to use.

How to Prepare Garlic for Cooking Use

To Peel a Clove

First, cut off the small stem end, and with the flat side of a chef's knife, press down on the clove until you hear a little crack. The garlic clove should now be easy to peel. Hard neck garlic is much easier to peel because of its thicker skin, whereas the soft neck cloves are much smaller and with finer skin.

Chopping or Crushing Garlic

The more finely garlic is chopped, the stronger the flavour of the garlic, as more of the garlic's cells have been broken, releasing the smell and taste for which it is known. It is said that chopping or crushing garlic with coarse salt brings out the flavour even more.

You may chop garlic using a chef's knife, garlic press or small grater. A food processor is not recommended as it is hardly worth the bother of cleaning the pieces for such a small quantity. Shops that sell kitchenware usually stock a wide array of garlic presses and garlic rasps which make mincing garlic much easier.

Finely chopped garlic also blends faster with your recipe ingredients and is easier to use. On the other hand, use larger pieces of garlic when making dishes that require a longer cooling time. The flavour here will dissipate more slowly.

Tips for Using Garlic

- Toss peeled garlic cloves onto your barbecue coals to help give your foods a zestier flavour.
- To remove the smell of garlic from your hands, rub your hands with toothpaste or rub them across a stainless steel sink.

All About Squash and Pumpkins

General Description

Squash, as well as pumpkins, are annuals in the gourd or Cucurbitaceae family. Cucumbers, watermelons and muskmelons are also members of the same family. Squash cultivation began with the Mayans of Mexico thousands of years ago. They are Western Hemisphere plants, grown long before any old world explorers ever arrived in these lands. Squash, however, has never attained much popularity in Europe, except in the warmer climates, such as Italy, where zucchini is popular. In England, squash is called "vegetable marrow." Nonetheless, over the centuries, squash have made their way to every part of the Americas. They are high in vitamin A, potassium, iron and riboflavin. In the fall, the squash and pumpkins are also high in vitamin C. Most commercially canned pumpkin contains the milder flavour squash.

There are two kinds of squash:

Summer squash are ready to be eaten in the summer. They theoretically are eaten when immature, or rather, when the skins are soft, an example being zucchini. Summer squash can be ripened and then cooked and eaten like winter squash.

Winter squash have a harder skin. The texture can be warty and rough. These squash originate from the Andes Mountains. Seeds are ripe for sowing. Winter squash require a longer growing season, as well as more growing space, than that of the summer variety. They have 1/2 to 1/3 the calories of a potato.

How to Grow Pumpkins and Squash

For outside planting: Plant the seeds at about the same time you would set out tomato or pepper plants (end of May to early June in the Ottawa area). Plant seeds in full sun in hills 6'–8' apart with approximately 6–7 seeds per hill. Do not plant when the forecast is for chilly weather, as the seeds are rather delicate and may not germinate. A forecast of excessive rain can also cause the seeds to rot. The seeds may also be started indoors 3–4 weeks earlier. To avoid transplant shock, start the seeds in peat pots or paper containers which can then be planted, pot and all, in the ground when the danger of frost is over.

Thin plants when seedlings are 3" high, in order to get the sweetest and meatiest fruits. They are heavy feeders and take up a lot of garden space. A light, fertile, well-drained soil with well-rotted manure and/or compost will help retain soil moisture.

An important time for watering is from bud development through to flowering. The plants need a lot of watering, especially up to mid-summer. Afterwards, the plant can do with less water. Even if a dry spell occurs after mid-summer and the leaves wilt, the plant is still sending energy to the fruit. They can endure a few weeks without water. At this time the plant will stop setting any more fruit, but with eventual watering it will recover. The fruit will be smaller but sweeter.

Each squash plant has both male and female flowers. Male blossoms are on the stems. They are slender all the way to the base, while the female blossoms end in a rounded bottom beneath the flower.

The more leaves on the squash or pumpkin plant, the better the yield, and some say the better the flavour. Squash plants generally send out one main vine. If you aim the squash plant as it grows, it will not get in your way. If the vines are getting out of hand, you may pinch off the ends once the vine has reached 4'. Your squash is ready for picking if when you press your thumb nail into the skin of the squash, it leaves no cut mark.

If you also plan on growing gourds, which are the decorative, non-edible small squash of many shapes and colours, do not plant them next to your squash or pumpkins as they may be cross-pollinated by bees, and cause your squash and pumpkins to become deformed and bitter. If you plan on collecting seeds for planting the following year, experts recommend that you do not grow more than one selection from each of the Maxima, Moschata or Pepo species, as the plants cross-pollinate and the result will be odd, misshapen fruit.

Squash and pumpkins are great plants for children to grow, as they grow rapidly and become spread out in the garden with huge fruits.

Preventive Tactics

If you see beetles and bugs on your plants, the best thing to do is to squash them (forgive the pun). Any sickly or ailing leaves should be thrown out in the garbage or burned, as they will infect other leaves and plants. Vines of squash can also mildew. This hinders whatever fruit is on that vine from growing any further. To avoid this, try not to water after 10 a.m. or get water on the leaves. Pumpkins and squash can develop a powdery mildew on the leaves later in the season which can affect the yield and storage of the crop. A mixture of 1 teaspoon of baking soda with 2 teaspoons of vegetable oil in 1 litre of water sprayed on the plants every 10 days and after each rain will help prevent this.

Harvesting

About 3 weeks before the first fall frost, begin pinching off any new tips, flowers or new fruit in order to give the older fruit a better chance to mature. Winter squash will not get overripe. A healthy vine will keep the fruit until it is ready to be harvested but it should be harvested before frost. The thicker-shelled squash will fare better in a light frost. Any immature squash on the vine after a frost will never mature as green tomatoes do. Simply dig them under or place them in your compost. When harvesting, leave 1" of stem on the fruit, making a clean cut.

Curing and Storing Winter Squash

Leave mature fruit on vine until rinds are hard. Then cure in the sun, or indoors in a warm, ventilated place for a week or so to thoroughly dry and harden the rinds. Then store in a single layer in a cool dry area, 13–16°C, such as a basement or root cellar. A cool closet in an unused bedroom may work fine.

Before storing, wipe fruits with a solution of 1 tablespoon chlorine (Javex) and 1 cup of water and then air dry. Store in a cool dark place. Don't stack them too much. Allow air to circulate around them. Every few weeks, check for rusty or black patches. Bring into kitchen, trim and cook and freeze the rest. As squash is stored over the winter months, its vitamin A content actually increases!

Buying

When buying your squash for storing, look at the stem to make sure it is dry and shrivelled-looking. This squash will store well as it was picked when mature on the vine. Select squash and pumpkins that are bright in colour and heavy for their size. The skin should not have soft, mouldy or rotten spots.

Freezing

To freeze, cut the squash in half and scrape out the stringy pulp. For the larger squash, you may need the help of a hammer to tap your knife through the tough skin. These halves or quarters may be microwaved for 10–30 minutes, depending on the size, or baked at 350°F on a buttered baking sheet for 30–50 minutes or until tender when pierced with a knife. Remove peel and purée in a food processor and place in freezer bags. In the fall when the oven is on more often, it is economical to add any squash or pumpkin that you wish to freeze by baking the fruit along with your favourite dish. When cool, place desired quantity in freezer bags and freeze. You may also freeze the squash freshly grated and/or cubed, ready for use in your favourite recipes.

Squash are classified into 3 areas: Maxima, Moschata and Pepo.

Maxima
- Skin colours are varied: orange, yellow, white, and green.
- Flesh is rich and deep-coloured.
- Vines are very long.
- Will keep up to 2 months in storage.
- The largest fruit of this family may weigh hundreds of pounds.
- These, however, are not good as jack-o'-lanterns.
- e.g.: turban, buttercup, Hubbard

Moschata
- Some believe these are the sweetest of the squash.
- Blossoms can be huge and beautiful.
- Leaves large and hairy but not prickly.
- Butternut is the most common and stores the longest.
- Sweet Potato is a favourite.
- We find here the oblong and tan pumpkins, not the round and orange.

Pepo
- Are as flavourful as they will ever be after harvest.
- Flesh is cream to orange-coloured.
- Fastest to mature but generally the shortest keeping.
- Must be eaten within a month of harvest.
- Leaves are prickly and may give you a rash.
- If raccoons are a problem getting into your corn, they will not come near this natural barbed-wire fence.
- We find here the pumpkins that we are familiar with: Halloween and pie
- e.g.: zucchini, acorn squash, spaghetti squash, most of the pumpkins

The More Popular Squash

Acorn

A small ribbed squash with a dark green skin and orange flesh, also known as pepper squash. It actually resembles an acorn. They can also have an orange skin. It matures the fastest of the Pepo squash family, and is a good variety to choose for short growing seasons. It has a pleasant flavour. When growing acorn squash, however, it is difficult to know when it is fully mature as it takes on its final colour before the flesh is fully sweet. In this case, follow the seed packet instructions. The average size is 1 to 1 1/2 lbs. It is ideal for baking and stuffing with filling. Acorn squash does not store as long as other types.

Buttercup

A squash that is slightly ribbed with a drum or turban shape having a raised bellybutton on the bottom. It has a darkish green skin colour with a pale dry flesh and the texture of a sweet potato. It is one of the most popular squash as far as flavour goes. Buttercup squash is good for steaming, puréeing or baking. The average size is 2 1/2 lbs.

Butternut

A long tan pear-shaped squash with a thick neck, warm orange flesh, and a small seed cavity at the base. The skin is very smooth. It is the most nutritious of the winter squash with nearly twice the beta-carotene and vitamin C. It stores very well. Butternut is a very versatile squash that is good in purées, soups and stews. The average size is 3–6 lbs.

Hubbard

Generally found in 3 colours: blue, green and orange. The blues can often grow to a watermelon size or as large as 25–30 lbs . Hubbards have a deep orange flesh. They have more or less a rounded shape with a tapered end, very much like a giant chocolate Hershey kiss. Hubbard squash stores very well and has one of the mildest flavours of all squash. It is best baked or steamed. The mid-size Hubbards have the best taste. They are often sold in supermarkets or produce stores pre-cut as the skin is rather thick. The average size is 8–10 lbs. Mini-Hubbards can weigh 2–3 lbs.

Spaghetti

This squash resembles a small yellow football. The skin is rather soft. The flesh, when cooked, separates into long "spaghetti-like" strands. Very mild and sweet-tasting. The average size is 3–6 lbs.

Turban

A squash with a flattened round base with three knobs resembling a colourful turban. The flesh is yellow to orange coloured. It is a variation of the buttercup squash. In recipes, it can be used interchangeably with the buttercup. It is great for use as a centerpiece or decoration. The average size is 3–6 lbs.

Notes

The Silver Spring
Farm Cookbook

*The Best of Garlic,
Squash, Pumpkins and Onions*

We hope you have enjoyed
The Silver Spring Farm Cookbook

If you would like to order additional copies for
friends and family, please complete this form
and send it to:

The Silver Spring Farm Cookbook
c/o Ottawa-Carleton Association for Persons
   with Developmental Disabilities (OCAPDD)
880 Wellington Street, Suite 200
Ottawa, Ontario K1R 6K7

Name: _____

Address: _____

_____

_____ Postal Code _____

Telephone Number: _____

Number of copies _____ @ $ 14.98 (GST included) = $ _____

Shipping and handling:
   $5.00 for one book + $1.00 for each
   additional book to a maximum of $10.00   = $ _____

                                    Total   = $ _____

VISA, Cheque or Money Orders are accepted.

VISA number _____

Exp. date: _____ Signature _____

Your book(s) will be sent by post. Please allow 2 – 3 weeks for delivery.